D1624340

THE SYRIA DILEMMA

THE SYRIA DILEMMA

edited by

Nader Hashemi and Danny Postel

A Boston Review Book

THE MIT PRESS Cambridge, Mass. London, England

MIT Press books may be purchased at special quantity discounts
for business or sales promotional use. For information, please
email special_sales@mitpress.mit.edu or write to Special Sales
Department, The MIT Press, 55 Hayward Street, Cambridge, MA
02142.

This book was set in Adobe Garamond by *Boston Review*
and was printed on recycled paper and bound in the United States
of America.

Library of Congress Cataloging-in-Publication Data

The Syria dilemma / edited by Nader Hashemi and Danny Postel.
    pages   cm.—(Boston review books)
Includes bibliographical references and index.
ISBN 978-0-262-02683-3 (hardcover : alk. paper)
1. Syria—History—Protests, 2011–2. Peace-building—
International cooperation. I. Hashemi, Nader, 1966– II. Postel,
Danny.
DS98.6.S94 2013
956.9104'2—dc23
                                                    2013024506

10   9   8   7   6   5   4   3   2   1

To the Syrian people

CONTENTS

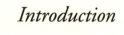

Introduction

Why Syria Matters

Nader Hashemi and Danny Postel

THE KILLING FIELDS OF SYRIA ARE RAPIDLY approaching those of Bosnia. According to the Office of the U.N. High Commissioner for Human Rights, 92,901 unique killings have occurred between March 2011 and April 2013, including 6,561 children.[1] Nearly two million have fled the country and 4.2 million have been internally displaced since the conflict began. "We have not seen a refugee outflow escalate at such a frightening rate since the Rwandan genocide almost 20 years ago," U.N. High Commissioner for Refugees Antonio Guterres said in July.[2] "After nearly two years, we no longer count days in hours, but in bodies," U.N. Secretary-General Ban Ki-moon has remarked. "Another day, another 100, 200, 300 dead. Fighting rages. Sectarian hatred is on the rise. The catalogue of war crimes is mounting."[3]

This rising tide of death has also been copiously documented by Amnesty International, Human Rights Watch, and the U.N. Independent International Commission on Inquiry on Syria. All have charged the Assad regime with a policy of state-sanctioned "war crimes" and "crimes against humanity" and the U.N. High Commissioner for Human Rights, Navi Pillay, has repeatedly called on the U.N. Security Council to refer Syria to the International Criminal Court (ICC). "We will be judged against the tragedy that has unfolded before our eyes," Pillay has stated.[4] Desmond Tutu, writing on behalf The Elders, a global network of prominent leaders on peace and human rights, has remarked that we are "all shamed by Syria's suffering."[5]

The nightmare in Syria has been front and center in the world's consciousness for over two years, but there is no consensus about what can—or should—be done to stop it. The U.N., the U.S., the European Union and the countries of the Middle East are flummoxed on how to end the conflict. Kofi Annan quit as U.N.-Arab League joint special envoy to Syria in frustration that his efforts came to naught. His successor, Lakhdar Brahimi, has been similarly exasperated, repeatedly threatening to step down. The Syrian conundrum evokes former U.S. Secretary of State Warren Christopher's description of the Bosnia war as "a problem from hell," a phrase etched in our moral and political lexicon by Samantha Power's Pulitzer-prize winning 2002 book.[6] And that phrase has made a comeback in the debate over Syria. In mid-2012 Anne-Marie Slaughter warned (in an essay reprinted in this volume) that if bold action wasn't taken quickly, Syria would become yet another problem from hell. The situation has only deteriorated since. The body count rises daily, with no end in sight. And the debate about what to do rages on.

Syria's Complexity

While the conflict in Syria has its origins in domestic politics—rooted in the corruption, nepotism, cronyism and repression of 42 years of Assad family rule—its regional and international dimensions are manifold. In this sense Syria is qualitatively different from and more complicated than the other Arab Spring rebellions, considering the multiplicity of actors who have a stake in the outcome of the conflict.[7]

Syria has morphed into a key battleground between Saudi Arabia and Iran for regional hegemony. Religious sectarianism, primarily promulgated by the Saudis and their allies, has risen to new heights and destabilized Lebanon and other neighboring countries in the process. Israel has entered the conflict to settle scores with Hezbollah and to indirectly send a message to Tehran. Turkey is deeply involved in Syria for its own reasons, and currently provides a home and safe haven for the Syrian opposition. Qatar's fingerprints are all over the conflict.[8]

Geopolitically, the Syrian conflict has led to new rivalries between the U.S., the U.K. and France on one side, and Russia and China on the other. The U.N. Security Council has been paralyzed as a result, with the non-permanent members dividing their support between these two camps. The first concrete sign of global cooperation to end the conflict emerged in May 2013, when it was announced that the US and Russia would jointly sponsor an international conference on Syria, based on the June 2012 final communiqué of the U.N.–backed Action Group for Syria meeting in Geneva.[9] While this process held some promise that global divisions over Syria might be narrowing, recent signs are unpromising. Both Russia and China are deeply invested in Syria and are using this issue to send a message that the West cannot unilaterally rewrite the rules and norms of international politics. Dmitri Trenin, Director of the Carnegie Endowment's Moscow Center, aptly observes that for Russia, "Syria is not primarily about Middle Eastern geopolitics, cold war-era alliances, arms sales—or even special interests. Syria, much like Libya, Iraq or Yugoslavia previously, is primarily about the world order. It's about who decides."[10]

The issue of Syria has been further complicated by the rise of radical Salafi-jihadi movements. While their numbers remain small, by all accounts their influence is growing. This is partly due to funding from Islamic charities in the Persian Gulf, as Thomas Pierret explains in his illuminating contribution to this book. But arguably the *absence* of significant support from the international community for the opposition's more democratic elements is equally critical. Whatever its causes, the growing Salafization of Syria's opposition has made the conflict even more intractable, a problem that will only deepen the longer the violence persists.[11]

Debating Intervention—Syria in the Shadow of Bosnia and Iraq

The debate over Syria is in many ways a flashback to the debates during the 1990s Balkan wars, not only because of the ethnic and religious divisions at work in the two conflicts but because of the arguments about intervention then and now.

The 1990s were the heyday of the humanitarian intervention paradigm. Somalia. Haiti. Bosnia. Kosovo. East Timor. The Responsibility to Protect (R2P). The case for international military forces stepping in to stop or prevent mass atrocities and crimes against humanity was all the rage in intellectual and policy circles. A cascade of books and articles elucidated the theoretical and practical dimensions of humanitarian intervention. It was the concept of the day.[12]

Then came Iraq. The catastrophe of the Iraq war seemed to have consigned the humanitarian intervention paradigm to the proverbial dustbin of history, and to have discredited its proponents, some (though by no means all) of whom signed on to that ill-fated invasion in the name of human rights.[13] The geopolitical tide seemed to have turned from humanitarian intervention to imperial hegemony, and cast a shadow of suspicion over the humanitarian interventionist idea.[14]

Syria has brought us back in many ways to the 1990s and the humanitarian intervention debate, as Libya had done on a smaller scale the year before. The mass killing has motivated many who advocated intervention to stop the bloodshed in the Balkans to do the same in Syria. In his essay for this volume, Michael Ignatieff, one of the leading proponents of humanitarian intervention in the 1990s, draws explicit connections between Bosnia and Syria.

But the shadow of Iraq very much looms over the Syria debate. Both the Iraq and Afghanistan wars have created deep and wide skepticism about military intervention, particularly led by the U.S. Iraq is a reference point for many opponents of intervention in Syria. In his contribution to this book, Fareed Zakaria invokes Iraq as a cautionary tale for why intervening in Syria would be futile and ill-conceived.

This view is widely shared in Washington policy circles. "In my meetings with American policy makers I often detect a conversation between ghosts," a senior Israeli diplomat has noted. "The ghosts of Afghanistan and Iraq are vying with the ghosts of Rwanda and Kosovo."[15]

Yet both Bosnia and Iraq can be argued the other way around in relation to Syria. In his essay in this volume, Shadi Hamid, in juxtaposition to Zakaria, contends that "Syria Is Not Iraq" and that the legacy of that war has confused the debate about what do to in Syria. And in juxtaposition to Ignatieff, Ambassador Christopher Hill draws on the process that ended the Bosnian conflict (one in which he played a critical role) to make the case for a diplomatic solution to the Syrian crisis.

Further complicating the picture, the Syria debate goes beyond conventional left/right categories. Many oppose intervening in Syria on conservative grounds. Realists and libertarians are among the most outspoken opponents of intervening in Syria. Liberal opinion is internally divided—as is the Obama administration itself.[16] Some liberals, like Anne-Marie Slaughter and Michael Ignatieff, favor intervention, while others, like Joe Klein and Marc Lynch, another contributor to this volume, oppose it.

Of course there are "noisy interventionists" like US senators John McCain and Lindsey Graham, whose agitations have given many liberals and anti-interventionists the impression that the case for intervening in Syria is some kind of neocon project. In fact things are more complicated— the neocons too are internally divided on Syria. While they would like to see Assad toppled, the specter of Islamist groups taking over has many neocons anxious and ambivalent about what the U.S. should do.[17]

The Left too is divided on Syria. Not between opponents and advocates of intervention—virtually no one on the Left favors military action in Syria. But there are significant divergences in perspective and interpretation: many leftists regard the Assad regime—at least in its regional role—in anti-imperialist terms, as part of the so-called axis of resistance against US and Israeli power, and are hostile to the Syrian opposition, while others on the Left support the Syrian uprising (albeit with deep reservations about the Islamist character of elements within it).[18]

The ideological fault lines of the Syria debate are complex and have created widespread confusion in multiple quarters. This state of affairs sent us on the quest that resulted in this book. In January 2013 we convened a conference on the Syrian crisis at the University of Denver. This volume grew partly out of that event. Several of the contributors to this volume participated in that gathering (though many did not). Our quest, in organizing that conference and subsequently in editing this book, was to assemble what we consider the most thoughtful perspectives on what should be done about the Syrian crisis.

In the pages that follow there are not two but several positions on that question. Some argue for arming the Syrian rebels, some against doing so. Some argue for intervention to topple the Assad regime, others against it. Mary Kaldor argues for an intervention aimed exclusively at protecting Syrian civilians. Kenneth Roth favors a humanitarian plan but not military intervention. It is not accidental that the contributors to this book disagree with one another. This array of contending perspectives reflects the profound dilemma that Syria confronts us with. Morally serious people sharply disagree over what should be done. There are compelling arguments on various sides of the issue. This book is by no means the final word on the ethical dilemma that Syria poses, but it is an invitation to critical engagement with that dilemma.

The Syria Dilemma

Syria Is Not Iraq: Why the Legacy of the Iraq War Keeps Us from Doing the Right Thing in Syria

TheAtlantic.com, February 4, 2013

Shadi Hamid

MORE THAN A YEAR AGO, A REAL DEBATE BEGAN over whether to intervene militarily in Syria. Here in *The Atlantic*, Steven Cook of the Council on Foreign Relations was one of the first to propose taking military action—or at least thinking seriously about it.[19] When Cook wrote his article (which, in its prescience, is well worth re-reading today), around 5,000 Syrians had been killed. Today, the number is more than 10 times that, and is now over 60,000 according to some estimates. I remember, early on, wondering whether 15,000 would be a "trigger."

But, apparently, there is no "trigger." Military intervention in Syria cannot happen without American support and there is nothing to suggest the United States has any interest in intervening, no matter the number of dead. The Obama administration has cited the use of chemical weapons as a "red line," but even that red line has managed to shift back and forth several times.

Opponents of intervention have, understandably, tended to focus on the risky—and potentially prohibitively difficult—nature of military action. Yet, the very fact that some "red lines" do exist suggests that the U.S. would be willing to intervene at some point, in spite of those difficulties. The question, then, isn't so much the difficulty of the operation as much as what is an appropriate red line.

If Bashar al-Assad proceeded to destroy an entire city, killing 100,000 people in a matter of weeks, presumably many of those opposing intervention would decide to support it. But why then and not now? Why exactly is 60,000 people not enough? Sure, the use of chemical weapons should be a red line for national security reasons, but why should strictly national security considerations be a red line, when the killing of tens of thousands is not?

It is this latter point which sends precisely the wrong message to Arab audiences and the broader international community. Nothing fundamental has changed in U.S. policy since the Arab Spring, even though many of us said, and hoped, that new realities required a new way of doing business. As I wrote nearly a year ago,

> What made Libya a "pure" intervention was that we acted not because our vital interests were threatened but in spite of the fact that they were not. For me, this was yet one more reason to laud it.[20]

The memory of the Iraq War obviously looms large. The war, itself, was one of the greatest strategic blunders in the recent history of American foreign policy. But its legacy is proving just as damaging, leading to a series of mistakes that we are likely to regret in due time. There would have been much more willingness to intervene in Syria if we hadn't intervened in Iraq. But the Bush Administraton's misguided adventurism abroad has made open displays of ideology, or even simple morality, in foreign policy seem suspect. Today, it is fashionable to play technocrat and ask "what works?" Asking this question, as opposed to others, is a marker of pragmatism and prudence. As difficult as it may be, the thinking goes, we must do away with moral sentiments and attachments, which tend to distort more than clarify.

As Cook pointed out in another piece, fundamental questions of morality and philosophy are what, in part, separate proponents and opponents of intervention. "Is it a morally superior position," Cook asks, "to sit by as people are being killed rather than take action that will kill people, but nevertheless may end up saving lives as well?"[21] The question here, then, isn't whether it will work, but will it be worth it?

Such questions are worth considering, and thinking seriously about, but they're unlikely to be resolved anytime soon. In returning to narrower questions of what, if anything, can stop the killing, a few considerations are in order. First, Bashar al-Assad might have a particularly high tolerance for brutality, but there is little to suggest he has ceased being a rational actor. And the unfortunate reality is that he has no real incentive to stop the slaughter of Syrians unless there is a credible threat of military action. It is clear that this is a relevant calculation for Assad and the people around him. The regime has spent the last year testing its limits, seeing how far it can go. Accordingly, the rate of killing has never dramatically shot up. Rather, it has increased slowly and gradually, as Assad gauges the international community's reactions and its willingness to intervene more aggressively. He apparently has gotten his answer.

Even if the Obama administration has little interest in intervening, it seems odd, even remarkable, that it would choose to telegraph that lack of interest to the Syrian regime in such a flagrant manner. It would have made much more sense for the Obama administration and leading European powers, along with NATO, to publicly discuss military options and make a good-faith effort to consider them.

So much of the aversion to intervention, as mentioned earlier, has been predicated on Syria's supposed similarity to Iraq and the fear of entering into another quagmire. But no one, to my knowledge, was proposing a full-on ground invasion of Syria. Instead, what was being suggested was an escalatory ladder of varying military options. An escalation would be contingent on how the Syrian regime (and the rebels) responded. Mission creep is always a risk, but if there was ever an administration resistant to mission creep, it is the Obama administration, as became evident during the Libya operation, when the U.S. went out of its way to limit its involvement, even at the cost of prolonging it.[22]

Another unfortunate feature of the ongoing debate was the tendency to treat the military option and the diplomatic "alternative" as mutually exclusive. They never were. On the contrary, they could have been pursued in parallel. In Bosnia, NATO power forced the Serbs to the negotiating table, leading to the Dayton Accords and the introduction of multinational peacekeeping forces. In Libya, the Qaddafi regime showed more interest in negotiating with the opposition after military intervention, rather than before (within a few weeks of the NATO operation, Qaddafi envoys were engaging in ceasefire talks).

Lastly, it is worth thinking about what this means for future instances of mass slaughter. With the Libya intervention, there was hope that a post-Arab Spring precedent would be set—that whenever pro-democracy protesters were threatened with massacre, the U.S. and its allies would take the "responsibility to protect" seriously and consider intervention as a legitimate option. But, nearly two years later, what we didn't do in Syria is more relevant than what we did do in Libya.

If I sound defeatist, it is likely because I am. It is worth speaking frankly, and, unfortunately, this probably requires speaking in the past tense. For Syria, it is likely too late. Notwithstanding something sudden and entirely unexpected, the international community will not intervene. That does not mean that the Syrian people are doomed. They will likely "win" in the end, but their victory, if we can even call it that, will have come at a much greater cost—in the sheer number killed—than was necessary. It will have come at the cost of a country destroyed, of sects polarized beyond any hope of reconciliation, of Salafis and Jihadists ascendant, of a state too torn and divided for real governance.

As has been reported elsewhere, the Syrian opposition feels that it has been not just forgotten, but, worse, betrayed. They are unlikely to forget this anytime soon. Anti-Americanism, a given among regime supporters, has slowly taken root among the opposition as well. The Syrian protest movement's Friday theme for October 19, 2012 was "America, has your spite not been sated by our blood?"

In due time, the Obama administration's inability or unwillingness to act may be remembered as one of the great strategic and moral blunders of recent de-cades. Hoping to atone for our sins in Iraq, we have overlearned the lessons of the last war. I only wish it wasn't too late.

Why There Is No Military Solution to the Syrian Conflict

Jadaliyya.com, May 13, 2013

Aslı Bâli and Aziz Rana

TODAY, AS VIOLENCE INTENSIFIES IN SYRIA, external powers, including the United States, are openly debating direct intervention. Such intervention is framed as serving multiple goals at once—as a means of securing chemical weapons caches, a mechanism to protect the civilian population, and a necessary measure to ensure that the successors to the Assad regime are adequately beholden to the U.S. and its regional allies.

But whether the intentions are humanitarian or strategic, policies of arming opposition groups, along with discussions of establishing "safe zones," using

Patriot missile batteries to enforce a "no-fly zone" and more direct calls for military intervention, are counterproductive at best, and at worst embody goals that further undermine the interests of the local population. If anything, it is intervention, not its absence, that fuels the blood-letting in Syria.

In fact, there is likely no form of direct or indirect military involvement in the conflict that will spare civilians or advance either side towards a decisive victory—there are too many interveners and too many strategic interests at stake for any side to allow too great a tipping of the balance. Some might argue that the ongoing destabilization of Syria serves its own strategic purposes. Aside from the deep moral bankruptcy of such a position, its logic of perpetual conflict threatens to engulf the region with spillover effects radiating beyond the control of potential interveners.

To appreciate why, look at events in Syria: An authoritarian regime is engaged in brutal repression and large-scale human rights atrocities. Indeed, there is no doubt the government of President Bashar al-Assad carries the overwhelming responsibility for the unfolding tragedy. But since international assistance began flowing to armed opposition groups in late 2011, the death and displacement to which civilians have been subjected has skyrocketed. At the end of the first year of the Syrian conflict, in April 2012, the United Nations estimated that 9,000 civilians had been killed. According to the U.N., the death toll a year later exceeds 70,000, with tens of thousands more wounded. The refugee count is set to top three million by the end of 2013.

Although a reflection of dynamics on the ground, the current stalemate is also, crucially, a product of an international standoff between the external and regional players—backers and opponents of the Assad regime. To date, external backers have focused on arming their local proxies rather than negotiating. Russia and Iran have reiterated their commitment to the Assad government, both diplomatically and through direct support. The United States has doubled down on supporting the rebels with military assistance in the form of "non-lethal" equipment (body armor, night vision goggles, armored vehicles and advanced communications systems), American training of Syrian insurgents in Jordan, and even the coordination of the flow of arms from Saudi Arabia, Qatar and Turkey to the Free Syrian Army. Recent reports suggest that the British and French are also contemplating sending weapons.

Problems With Intervention

The current confrontational approach is unsurprising, because toppling the Syrian regime would alter the regional balance of power against Iran and in favor of pro-Western governments. Until quite recently the United States was prepared to partner with the Assad regime, however repressive: the country played a well-documented role in the United States' extraordinary rendition of terrorism suspects. But today Syria presents a low-cost opportunity to shift regional alliances while appearing to intervene in support of popular demands for regime change.

In fact, capitalizing on a perceived opportunity in Syria is the opposite of responsiveness to local demands—it is an attempt to control outcomes from outside and one that will be more costly in the long run than most analysts suppose. As for the short run, such policies centered on military assistance have contributed to a drawn-out and increasingly bloody civil war.

As the record from the second year of the Syrian conflict demonstrates, the rebels have begun to achieve parity with the military through indiscriminate armed attacks, often resulting in as many casualties among civilians as among the ostensible targets. Even with additional arms, opposition groups resisting Assad's repression may fight the regime to a standstill only.

Further, arguments for increased military assistance to the armed opposition miss political complexities within Syria. On one side, large sections of the country oppose President Assad, and a significant proportion back efforts of armed rebel groups to topple his government. In cities like Homs and Dara'a, regime brutality consolidated support for rebels from the outset. Elsewhere, in major cities like Damascus and Aleppo, and in the coastal towns of Latakia and Tartus, the picture has been more mixed. Some neighborhoods supported a network of anti-government protest organizers known as the Local Coordination Committees; others backed militants.

But many sectors of society—including most minority groups like the Christians, Druze and Alawites, along with much of the middle class and business owners—initially withheld support from the rebels. The most likely explanation was that they feared more instability and violence, as well as some possible outcomes, like rule by Islamist actors. The rebel incursion into Aleppo in July 2012 did little to quell these fears, with brutal fighting on all sides leaving emptied and battle-scarred neighborhoods. Caught between a military onslaught by the government and rebel attacks, almost the entirety of Aleppo's large Christian community has fled the city and the country.

The demographic makeup of Aleppo and many other mixed communities across the country is rapidly being transformed by the sectarianization of the conflict, driven as much by the regional supporters supplying both the government and the armed rebel forces as by internal dynamics. The intensification of the battle for Damascus will likely produce a similar result as the summer of 2013 sets in. Indeed, with urban areas, provincial towns, and even rural villages emptied of their populations, the fighting has accelerated and social fragmentation has been exacerbated. To underscore the point, even shifting dynamics on the ground marking rebel advances have not eased such fragmentation—a fact that belies the argument that nearly all segments of the civilian population would welcome direct external intervention on behalf of armed opposition groups.

Given these realities, repeated discussions of new, more coercive military options, especially against the backdrop of concerns about the use of chemical weapons by the regime, risk worsening the situation. Allegations of chemical weapons use, while horrifying, concern a tiny proportion of total civilian casualties in the conflict. Direct intervention to secure or destroy chemical weapons caches will do little to address the principal armed threat facing civilians. In order to defeat the regime militarily, the United States and its allies would have to dramatically heighten the magnitude of destruction wrought on the country, resulting in greater civilian casualties. It may set the stage for escalating internecine conflict not only pitting Sunni constituencies backed by Turkey, Saudi Arabia and Qatar against opponents that they increasingly identify in sectarian or ethnic terms, but also consuming neighborhoods in inter-militia wars. The result would be a deeply destabilized Syria bordering on Israel, Turkey, Jordan, Iraq and Lebanon, creating the potential for a long-term proxy war between regional Sunni and Shia political forces. The eventual outcome would have no clear winner but a multitude of losers, most crucially ordinary Syrian civilians.

Contours of a Diplomatic Approach

Still, there remains a chance for the international community to contribute to a transition process that ensures the security of all communities—including regime backers—ending violence in exchange for Assad's departure. But pursuing regime decapitation through military escalation will not produce such a process. Ultimately, the best way for external actors to help reduce violence is to support negotiations for a political transition that would include rather than explicitly threaten elements of the regime. Given the existential fears of communities on each side of the conflict, the first goal has to be making clear that all groups have a future in a new Syria.

The United Nations might yet prove a useful intermediary. Though mediation efforts led by Kofi Annan failed, this was in large part because major powers were pursuing a militarization strategy rather than a negotiated solution. Lakhdar Brahimi, Annan's successor, has sought to maintain the possibility of diplomatic engagement, though often expressing frustration that his mandate is undermined as parties continue to support an armed approach. Brahimi's most recent call for a weapons embargo on all sides is an opportunity to end the double-speak, in which actors maintain their desire to engage in talks while nonetheless ramping up violence on the ground.

Still, for a political solution to be viable a weapons embargo would be a necessary but insufficient first step. Crucially, real negotiations would have to encompass not only all the internal parties but also *all* the external actors involved, including Iran and Russia. Both have stakes in the Assad government; their participation in an inclusive mediation process could set the stage for concessions by the government.

For all of the problems with "managed transition" in Yemen, the removal of Ali Abdallah Saleh from power in 2012 highlighted just the kind of pressure that can be brought to bear on a regime by its principal supporters. This suggests that Iranian and Russian action may well succeed in removing Assad where force from hostile outsiders has so far failed. In Yemen, the regime's supporters (including the United States) ultimately conceded to protesters' demands by enabling Saleh to step down only after assuring their interests were secure.

There is no reason to expect that the Assad regime's principal sponsors would participate in an international strategy that results in dispatching their ally unless they are also convinced that their interest in a regional sphere of influence will not thereby be harmed (or at any event that the costs to them of the internationally sanctioned plan are no higher than the best alternatives from their perspective). The principal obstacle to engagement with Iran and Russia has been American opposition. Yet opportunities for creative diplomacy with these countries provide a potential path forward. In the case of Russia, this may mean something along the lines of continued guaranteed access to warmwater ports on Syria's Mediterranean coast. In Iran's case, inducements may take the form of concessions related to sanctions and the current P5+1 talks on the nuclear file.

Some will argue that the US or the international community shouldn't negotiate seriously with the Syrian government or its backers. But by relying exclusively on coercion through sanctions, arming opposition groups, and threats, the practical effect of the current approach has been to squeeze out all diplomatic options and make a proxy war (with local and international players on both sides) the only remaining possibility. That strategy has produced more war, more civilian death, and more refugees. But in over two years it has not sufficiently shifted the military balance of forces on the ground to enable either side to establish a decisive military advantage.

The Challenge Ahead

We appreciate the difficulties of a peaceful resolution. It ultimately may be the case that the various forces on the ground are unwilling to negotiate a compromise that avoids still greater bloodshed. In particular, some opposition groups may find it unacceptable to enter into a bargain with elements of the Assad regime. But that choice is not one that should be determined in advance by outside actors, especially through externally-produced incentives to pursue military victory at all costs. Due to the civilian cost to date and the likely consequences of more violence, we believe it is incumbent on the international community to pursue all available diplomatic options, including real engagement with Iran.

But the failure to take diplomacy seriously underscores a profound moral hazard generated by the international community's prevailing framework. While basic international commitments to provide humanitarian assistance to Syrian refugees and internally displaced populations have been honored in the breach, external actors fulfill and exceed their pledges of military support. It is not credible to suggest that the international community is animated by humanitarian concerns and supports an end to the conflict at the same time that major powers are sustaining the current stalemate by arming and financing military factions on all sides.

In a sense, there is a tautology at work in current international approaches. Through covert and overt forms of military assistance, all parties are employing strategies that underscore that war is the only potentially winning option. And then, precisely because of the effects of these strategies, both international and local actors reject a diplomatic solution out of hand as an impossibility. Even worse, external policies lead domestic factions to imagine that victory remains on the horizon when circumstances suggest otherwise.

Indeed, as the violence continues to escalate, the real likelihood exists of ongoing bloody urban combat. The regime's cohesiveness may fray, but regime elements will not simply disappear. Rather, the military and security apparatus may fragment into their own large militias, possibly retrenching around rump territory. With Damascus on the brink of destruction, a protracted military stalemate rather than a clean overthrow of the regime is a foreseeable medium-term scenario. But despite the absence of a clear means for ending the conflict militarily, pledges of armed support reinforce the illusion that complete victory—by reaching an internal "tipping point"—might be possible without any compromises or accommodations.

In resigning as special envoy to Syria, Kofi Annan drew attention to the urgent need for diplomacy, not clandestine intervention. Because this warning has gone unheeded, Annan's replacement, Lakhdar Brahimi, has yet to find any other way out of a lengthy civil war of devastating proportions—devastating both for the Syrian people and for the Middle East as a whole. If the international community is interested in protecting the civilian population, the benefits of a negotiated transition are clear. Diplomatic engagement may not have the allure of humanitarian rescue or serve the strategic goal of flipping regional alliances. But it is far more likely than any of the current options on the table to actually safeguard ordinary Syrians and to create the political space that might facilitate a locally-directed outcome.

Bosnia and Syria: Intervention Then and Now
Michael Ignatieff

WHEN STATE ORDER COLLAPSES, AS IT DID IN Yugoslavia in the 1990s, as it is doing now in Syria, chaos unleashes existential fear among all the groups who had once sheltered under the protection of the state. Such fear makes it difficult to sustain multi-confessional, pluralist, tolerant orders when dictatorship falls apart. When state order collapses, every confessional or ethnic group asks one question: who will protect us now?[23]

As Sunni, Alawite, Christian, Druze and Shia ask this question, they know the only possible answer is themselves. In a Hobbesian situation—a war of all against all—each individual gravitates back to the security offered by their clan, sect or ethnic group, or more precisely, to those individuals within those groups who offer armed protection. This is especially the case when dictatorships collapse, for in this case a security vacuum emerges on top of a political one. In a state that never permitted mobilization of political parties across sectarian, clan, or ethnic divides, none of these groups has learned to trust each other in a political order. They may share a hatred of the dictator and a fear of what comes next, but not much else. Politics has never brought them together before. Now they are faced with security dilemmas and they conclude, rationally enough, that they can only face these dilemmas alone, in the safety of their own group. Such was the case in the former Yugoslavia. Such is the case now in Syria.

In listening to the Syrian opposition figures who have fought courageously to create a pluralist, multi-confessional democratic Syria upon the ruins of the Assad regime, I am struck by how much they sound like Yugoslavs, especially the Bosniaks of the early 1990s. They too sought to create a post-ethnic politics after Tito's death. They too sought to preserve the complex, multi-confessional heritage of tolerance that many in the Syrian opposition are struggling to preserve. These ideals are not abstractions. These Syrian patriots actually lived a Syrian identity beyond confessional divisions. The lesson from Yugoslavia is how difficult it is to sustain these connections and a common identity in the face of the fear that overcomes all ethnic groups upon the collapse of state order. Common identities and loyalties rarely survive the rush to the protection of armed groups and the bitterness that results when these groups begin killing each other. Neither the Yugoslavs of the 1990s nor Syrians today are trapped in sectarian, Islamist 'fanatical' or 'primitive' or 'archaic' emotions (to quote some of the condescending terms that outsiders used to describe the hatreds that tore Yugoslavia apart). What they both lack is time, the experience of democracy, and the opportunity—it can take generations—to forge political alliances across confessional, sectarian, and clan lines. This was the legacy of dictatorship that Tito bequeathed to Yugoslavia and it is Assad's poisonous gift to Syria. No wonder then that it has proved agonizingly difficult for the Syrian opposition to create a common front against the dictator and a political program for their country after Assad is defeated, killed, or driven into exile. No wonder then that the chief casualty of the Assad regime might just be Syria itself.

Such an analysis helps us to explain why the anti-Assad opposition has been unable to create a believable government in exile linked both to commanders at the front and to the municipal authorities in the liberated zones. Inside and outside, exiles and front-line fighters regard each other with suspicion. There is no effective national command of the insurrection and hence no shared political claim to defend together. In addition there are a number of fighters, the al Nusra Brigade being only one example, for whom the goal is not the defense of a multi-confessional

Syria but the creation of an Islamic caliphate in Arab lands. As Western governments have considered their options since the uprising began, they have found it easier to identify those they want to lose than those they want to win.

Intervention will not occur until interveners can identify with a cause that democratic electorates in Western states can make their own. In the former Yugoslavia it was the Bosniak Sarajevans who understood this clearly and helped to mobilize the outrage in Western countries that eventually made intervention possible. They had always stood for a tolerant, multi-confessional city and in retrospect they did a heroic job in making their cause Europe's own. Intervention finally occurred in 1995, at least in some measure because international opinion identified the Bosniaks as a worthy victim who could be assisted in the name of a general defense of 'European values.' The massacre in Srebrenica and the market bombing in Sarajevo were triggers for intervention, but the ideological ground had been prepared in the West by

Sarajevan suffering in the siege. For the moment, the Syrian opposition has failed in making their cause a universal claim.

The Western intervention in Bosnia—air-strikes on Bosnian Serb targets, clandestine assistance to Croatian and Bosniak units who then drove Serb minorities from Croatian and Bosnian territory—brought the parties to Dayton in October 1995.[24] There Richard Holbrooke negotiated a peace that preserved Bosnia-Hercegovina as a state and forced institution sharing upon unwilling enemies. Western intervention did not succeed in recreating the inter-ethnic tolerance and accommodation. It may only have locked ethnic hostility in place, but it did force ethnic groups to deal with each other politically and to accept, over time, that limited co-operation was a better option than war. The fact remains that no one is dying in Bosnia today.

When Western governments consider Syrian pleas for intervention, it is not Bosnia that comes to their minds, but Iraq, Afghanistan, and Libya. The decade of interventions that began after 9/11 appears to deliver only lessons of futility and perversity. A decade later both Iraq and Afghanistan rank as failed states. In Libya, Qaddafi may be gone, but power remains in the hands of militias. Moreover, once Qaddafi's arms flowed out into the Sahara to the Tuareg and al Qaeda in the Maghreb, they were able to take their uprising against the state of Mali to within striking distance of the capital, forcing a French intervention. Anyone contemplating intervention in Syria has to prevent unintended consequences like these, especially the leakage of Syrian chemical and biological weapons stocks to al Qaeda affiliates.

Libya, Iraq and Afghanistan only partly explain why such domestic support as once existed for "humanitarian intervention" has disappeared. Life has also changed for the intervening states themselves. The interventions in Bosnia—and later in Kosovo— were the work of a different time. They were discretionary affairs, small wars of choice that were easily paid for by expansive European and North American societies whose economies were growing robustly. The political confidence that led to these operations depended on budgetary surpluses and on euphoric confidence in the superiority of the Western democratic model in the unipolar moment that followed the collapse of the Soviet Empire. In the current age of sequester, austerity and deficit, this confidence has vanished. Europe's political elites are exclusively focused on the survival of their economic and political union. The United States, likewise, is struggling with deficits, austerity and recession. To recession-weary democratic publics, nation-building at home seems a more defensible project than nation-building abroad.

In this climate of reduced expectation, a risk-averse form of Realism has taken hold of Western capitals, particularly Washington. Realist proponents ask, what interest does the United States actually have in intervening in Syria at all? Or more pungently, who cares which bunch of thugs runs the country?[25] These are necessary questions and the failure to ask them over Iraq in 2002 led to disaster. After Iraq, the lesson learned has been no more wars of choice, only wars of necessity. The wars of necessity that command reluctant democratic assent in the U.S. are now the drone strikes in Yemen and Pakistan.

It is a sign of the new climate of opinion that when asked about Syria, Obama replied, "Why Syria, why not Congo?"[26] The President's rhetorical question implied its own answer. Humanitarian suffering alone constitutes no clear principle of triage, and it is a president's job to do triage, to apportion scarce national resources and scarcer political capital to a few vital tasks. Bloodshed and carnage alone will not—and should not—trigger the dispatch of the Marines.

It follows, unfortunately, that if seventy thousand deaths in the Syrian civil war have not created the political will to intervene, there is no good reason to suppose that double that number will have any more effect. The Lebanese civil war burned for twenty years. It is not impossible to anticipate the same result in Syria—and for similar reasons. In both Lebanon and Syria, and unlike in Bosnia, external Western interveners have been unable to identify a side whose victory would further their interests.

Western policy is navigating between Scylla and Charybdis. Aligning with the Russians to prop up Assad would be both unconscionable and futile. Invading Syria would reproduce the folly of Iraq. The policy alternative in the middle, between these two options, is hard to define because the Syrian rebels do not constitute either a united front or a believable alternative to the Assad regime. There are no good guys, no victims whose cause can be sold to reluctant publics to ennoble a humanitarian rescue. So little has been done by Washington to aid the rebels that the policy—high on rhetoric, low on action—reads like a further indication—if the failure to move Israel and Palestine towards peace weren't enough indication already—of reduced American influence in the entire Middle East. For the Realists, facing up to the decisive limits of American power in the region is the beginning of wisdom. For others, Realism looks like abandonment.

Can it really be true that the United States and its allies in the region have no strategic interest in which group of thugs eventually rules Syria? Can it really be true that America will suffer no consequences in the "Arab street" for standing by while tens of thousands of Syrians are killed by their own regime? Is it in America's interest for Syria to collapse and become a failed state? To pose these as rhetorical questions is to suggest the answers. Syria matters, and its future matters not only to itself and its people but to an entire region and to Western interests there.

Apparently after much internal debate the Obama administration has concluded that Syria does matter. Lethal and non-lethal aid is being funneled to Syrian fighters, through Turkey and through Jordan, under the watchful eye of the CIA.[27] Further assistance is reaching the fighters through Saudi Arabia and the Gulf states. The purpose of arms transfer is political as much as it is military. Its intent is to give the U.S. and its allies some leverage over the groups who receive the arms. The leverage, presumably, will be applied to induce the Syrian opposition to behave like a government in waiting and to act like one when Assad falls. Acting like a government would mean doing whatever it can to preserve the territorial integrity of Syria and to prevent a wave of revenge killings against minorities, particularly the Alawites. Behaving like a government would mean initiating an inclusive constitutional process that would give a fractured society a chance to heal and come together. Behaving like a government would mean accepting U.N. peacekeepers to give the society the chance to hold violence-free elections.

The question no one can answer is whether external aid has come too late to confer any leverage at all, as the rebels close in and the final battles for Damascus get underway. The same question hovers over the increasing flow of aid to civilian authorities and municipalities in the liberated zones of Syria. What leverage can the U.S. hope to exert over the post-Assad landscape when aid has been so little and so late? The decisive gesture, of course, would be for the United States to interdict Assad's use of air power, possibly through the activation of the Patriot batteries in Turkey. Thus far, there is no evidence that the U.S. is ready to take this step, and its hesitation is a mixture of risk aversion and strategic calculation. The Syrian crisis has dug the Russians and Chinese ever more deeply into their opposition to any U.N. Security Council authorization of the use of force, and so the Americans face a lesser-evil choice. Interdiction of Assad's air power would collapse the Assad regime, but it would also jeopardize the support America needs from these powers in its ongoing duel with the Iranians. America will have to decide whether it needs China and Russia more than it needs leverage over post-Assad Syria and the new landscape in the region.

Nearly twenty years ago, as the intervention in Bosnia came together, the geo-strategic order looked very different. The Russian state was near collapse and the Chinese were cautiously edging their way out into the international arena. Neither stood in the way of intervention in Bosnia. Today, the Syrian crisis lays bare the contours of a very different world: divided between authoritarian crony capitalist oligarchies that have set themselves against any form of international intervention in sovereign states and distracted, deficit-ridden democracies that lack the will or capacity to shape even a region as strategic as the Middle East. The Syrians huddling under tents in Lebanon, Jordan and Turkey, the families queuing for bread in free Aleppo while scanning the sky for planes overhead, the fighters taking on a dictator's tanks—they are the ones paying the price for this divided world. They are the ones now thinking that they have been abandoned. If they win their freedom, they will have no reason to thank us and they will have no inclination, as they settle their scores, to listen to anything the West, or anyone else, has to say. We should will them on to victory, but due to our inability to act consequently in their defense, we have reason to wonder whether Syria will survive once they win.

What Should Be Done About the Syrian Tragedy?
Citizen Pilgrimage, January 19, 2013

Richard Falk

Ever since the Vietnam War I have viewed all Western claims to use force in the post-colonial non-West with suspicion. I support presumptions in favor of non-intervention and self-determination, both fundamental norms of international law.

But in January I attended the full-day conference on "Resolving the Syria Crisis" that Nader Hashemi and Danny Postel convened at the University of Denver, and I left dissatisfied with my position that nothing more could or should be done at the international level to help end the violence in Syria or to assist the struggle of the Syrian people. I became convinced that human solidarity with the ordeal of the Syrian people was being deeply compromised by the advocacy of passivity in the face of the persisting criminality of the Damascus government, although dilemmas remain as to discerning a genuinely constructive course of action. To stand by is unacceptable, but to act without some realistic prospect of improving the situation is equally unacceptable.

In the immediate background of the debate on Syrian policy are the bad memories of stealth diplomacy used by the United States and several European partners in March 2011 to gain U.N. Security Council backing for the establishment of a No Fly Zone to protect the beleaguered and endangered population of the Libyan city of Benghazi. What ensued from the outset of the U.N.-authorized mission in Libya was a blatant disregard of the limited mandate to protect the population of a city from a threatened massacre. In its place, the NATO undertaking embarked on a concerted regime-changing mission that ended with the unseemly execution of the Libyan dictator. What

NATO purported to do was not only oblivious to Libya's sovereignty; it was unmistakably a deliberate and dramatic expansion of the authorized mission that understandably infuriated the autocrats in Moscow, and undermined confidence in Security Council procedures. A case could certainly have been made that in order to protect the Libyan people it was necessary to rid the country of the Qaddafi regime, but such an argument was never developed in the Security Council debate, and would never have been accepted. Against this background, the wide gap between what was approved by the U.N. Security Council vote and what was done in breach of the mandate was perceived as a betrayal of trust in the setting of the Security Council, particularly by those five governments opposed to issuing a broader writ for the intervention—governments that had been deceptively induced to abstain on the grounds that the U.N. authorization of force was limited to a single, well-delineated, protective, emergency mission.

Global diplomacy being what it was—and is—

there should be no surprise, and certainly no condescending, self-righteous lectures delivered by Western diplomats, in reaction to the rejectionist postures adopted by Russia and China throughout the Syrian crisis. Of course, two wrongs hardly ever make a right, and do not here. NATO's flagrant abuse of the U.N. mandate for Libya should certainly not be redressed at the expense of the Syrian people. In this respect, it is lamentable that those who shape policy in Moscow and Beijing are displaying indifference to the severity of massive crimes against humanity, principally perpetrated by the Assad government, as well as to the catastrophic national and regional effects of a continuing large-scale civil war in Syria. The unfolding Syrian tragedy, already resulting in more than 70,000 confirmed deaths, over one million refugees, as many as 3 million internally displaced, a raging famine, daily hardships and hazards for most of the population, and widespread urban devastation, seems almost certain to continue in coming months. There exists even a distinct possibility of an intensification of violence as a deciding battle for control of Damascus gets underway in a major way. Minimally responsible behavior by every leading government at the U.N. would, under such circumstances, entail at the very least a shared and credible willingness to forego geopolitical posturing, and exert all possible pressure to bring the violence to an end.

Some suggest that an effect of this geopolitical gridlock at the U.N. is causing many Syrians to sacrifice their lives and put the very existence of their country in jeopardy. This kind of "compensation" for NATO's *ultra vires* behavior in Libya is morally unacceptable and politically imprudent. At the same time it is hardly reasonable to assume that the U.N. could have ended the Syrian strife in an appropriate way if the Security Council had been able to speak with one voice. It both overestimates the capabilities of the U.N. and under-appreciates the complexity of the Syrian struggle. Under these circumstances it is diversionary to offload the frustrations associated with not being able to do anything effective to help the rebel forces win quickly, or to impose a ceasefire and political process, on the stubborn insistence by Russia and China that a solution for Syria must not be based on throwing Assad under the bus.

The Syrian conflict seems best interpreted as a matter of life or death not only for the ruling regime, but for the entire Alawite community (estimated to be 12 percent of the Syrian population of about 23 million), along with their support among Syria's other large minorities (Christian 10 percent, Druze 3 percent), and a sizable chunk of the urban business world that apparently fears more what is likely to follow Assad than Assad himself.

Given these conditions, there is little reason to assume that a unified posture among the permanent members of the Security Council would at any stage in the conflict have had any realistic prospect of bringing the Syrian parties to drop their weapons and agree to risk a supervised ceasefire. The origins of the crossover from militant anti-regime demonstrations to armed insurgency is most convincingly traced back to the use of live ammunition by the governing authorities and the armed forces against demonstrators in the city of Daraa from March 15, 2012 onwards, resulting in several deaths. Many in the streets of Daraa were arrested, with confirmed reports of torture and summary execution, and from this point forward there has been no credible turning away from violence by either side. Kofi Annan, who resigned as U.N.-Arab League joint Special Envoy to Syria in late January 2013, indicated his displeasure with both external and internal actors, criticizing Washington for its insistence that any political transition in Syria must be preceded by the removal of Assad from power, a precondition that seems predicated on an insurgent victory rather than working for a negotiated solution.

Without greater diplomatic pressure from both geopolitical proxies, the war in Syria is likely to go on and on with increasingly disastrous results. There has never been a serious willingness to solve the problems of Syria by an American-led attack in the style of Iraq 2003. For one thing, an effective intervention and occupation in a country the size of Syria, especially if both sides have significant levels of support as they continue to have, would be costly in lives and resources, uncertain in its overall effects on the internal balance of forces, and involve an international commitment that might last more than a decade. Especially in light of Western experiences in Iraq and Afghanistan, neither Washington nor Europe has the political will to undertake such an open-ended mission, especially when the perceived strategic interests are ambiguous and the political outcome is in doubt. Besides, 9/11 has receded in relevance (although still insufficiently) and the Obama foreign policy, while being far too militaristic, is much less so than the foreign policy of George W. Bush.

Another approach would be to press harder for an insurgent victory by tightening sanctions on Syria or combining a weapons embargo on the regime with the supply of weapons to the opposition. This also seems difficult to pull off, and highly unlikely to bring about a positive outcome even if feasible. It is difficult to manage such an orchestration of the conflict in a manner that is effective, especially when there are strong proxy supporters on each side. Furthermore, despite much external political encouragement, especially by Turkey, the anti-Assad forces have been unable to generate any kind of leadership that is widely acknowledged either internally or externally; nor has the opposition been able to project a shared vision of a post-Assad Syria. The opposition is clearly split between secular and Islamist orientations, which heightens the sense of not knowing what to expect on "the day after." We have no reliable way of knowing whether escalating assistance to the rebels would be effective, and if so, what sort of governing process would emerge in Syria, and to what extent it would be abusive toward those who directly and indirectly sided with the government during the struggle.

Under such circumstances seeking a ceasefire and negotiations between the parties still seems like the most sensible alternative among an array of bad options. This kind of emphasis has guided the diplomatic efforts of the U.N.-Arab League joint Special Envoys to Syria—first Kofi Annan and now Lakhdar Brahimi—but so far producing only disillusionment. Neither side seems ready to abandon the battlefield, partly because of enmity and distrust, and partly because it still is unwilling to settle for anything less than victory. For diplomacy to have any chance of success would appear to require both sides to entertain seriously the belief that a further continuation of the struggle is more threatening than ending it. It is tragic that such a point has not been reached, and indeed is not even in sight.

Despite the logic behind these failed efforts, to continue to pin hopes on this passive diplomacy under U.N. auspices seems problematic. It grants the governing Assad regime time and space to continue to use means at its disposal to destroy its internal enemy, relying on high technology weaponry and indiscriminate tactics on a vast scale that are killing and terrifying far more civilians than combatants. Bombarding

residential neighborhoods in Syrian cities with modern aircraft and artillery makes the survival of the regime appear far more significant for the rulers than is
any commitment to the security and wellbeing of the
Syrian people, and even the survival of the country
as a viable whole. It is deeply delegitimizing, and is
generating a growing chorus of demands for indict-
ing the Assad leadership for international crimes even
while the civil war rages on. This criminal behavior
expresses such an acute collective alienation on the
part of the Damascus leadership as to forfeit the normal rights enjoyed by a territorial sovereign. These
normal rights include the option of using force in ac-
cord with international humanitarian law to suppress
an internal uprising or insurgency, but such rights do
not extend to the commission of genocidal crimes
of the sort attributable to the Assad regime in recent
months. It must be acknowledged that the picture
is complicated by the realization that not all of the
criminal wrongdoing is on the regime side, yet the
great preponderance seems to be. The rebel forces, to

be sure, are guilty of several disturbing atrocities. This is sad and unfortunate, as well as politically confusing so far as taking sides is concerned. It merely adds to the victimization of the Syrian people, which is reaching catastrophic proportions, because it makes more difficult the mobilization of international support for concerted action.

Essentially, the world shamelessly watches the Syrian debacle in stunned silence, but is it fair to ask what could be done that is not being done? So far no credible pro-active international scenario has emerged. There are sensible suggestions for establishing local ceasefires in the considerable areas in the countryside under the control of rebel forces, for supplying food and medical supplies to the population by means of protected "humanitarian corridors," and for taking steps to improve the woeful lot of Syrian refugees currently facing inadequate accommodations and unacceptable hardships in Lebanon and Jordan. Such steps should be taken, but are unlikely to hasten or alter outcome of the conflict. Can more be done?

I would further recommend a broad policy of support for civil society activists within Syria and outside who are dedicated to a democratic and inclusive governing process that affirms human rights for all, and promises constitutional arrangements that will privilege no one ethnic or religious identity and will give priority to the protection of minorities. There are encouraging efforts underway by networks of Syrian activists, working mainly from Washington and Istanbul, to project such a vision as a program in the form of a Freedom Charter that aspires to establish a common platform for a future beneficial for all of Syria's people. The odds of success for this endeavor of politics from below seem remote at present, but they deserve our support and confidence.

As is often the case when normal politics are paralyzed, the only solution for this type of deadly encounter appears to be utopian until it somehow materializes and becomes history. This dynamic was illustrated by the benign unraveling of South African apartheid in the early 1990s against all odds, and in opposition to a consensus among experts that expected emancipation of the victims of apartheid to come, if at all, only by means of a long and bloody war.

Another initiative that could be taken, with great positive potential, but against the grain of current Western—especially American—geostrategy, would be to take the Iran war option off the table. Such a step would almost certainly have major tension-reducing effects in relation to regional diplomacy, and would be a desirable initiative quite independent of the Syrian conflict. The best way to do this would be to join with other governments in the region, including Iran, to sponsor a comprehensive security framework for the Middle East that features a nuclear weapons free zone, with an insistence that Israel join in the process. Of course, for the United States to advocate such moves would be to shake the foundations of its unconditional endorsement of whatever Israel favors and does, and yet it would seem over time to be of even greater benefit to Israeli security than an engagement in a permanent struggle to maintain

Israeli military dominance in the region while denying the right of self-determination to the Palestinian people. If American leaders could finally bring themselves to serve the national interest of the United States by acting as if the peace and security of Israel can only be achieved if the rights of the Palestinian people under international law are finally realized, it would be likely to have many positive effects for the Middle East and beyond. As matters now stand, the dismal situation in the region is underscored by the degree to which such prudent proposals remain in the domain of the unthinkable, and are kept outside the disciplined boundaries of "responsible debate."

If the imagination of the political is limited to the "art of the possible" then constructive responses to the Syrian tragedy seem all but foreclosed. Only what appears to be currently implausible has any prospect of providing the Syrian people and their nation with a hopeful future, and we need the moral fortitude to engage with what we believe is right even if we cannot demonstrate in advance that it will prevail in the end.

Anxiously Anticipating a New Dawn:
Voices of Syrian Activists

Afra Jalabi

THIS ESSAY IS AN ATTEMPT TO PRESENT THE perspectives of a range of Syrian civil society activists from varying backgrounds and give voice to their struggles with the question of what is the solution to the nightmare they are living through. Despite the bleak conditions they are confronting, these activists maintain the ethos that started the Syrian revolution and keep it going, and express views that could spare the country yet further destruction.

While visiting the liberated areas around the countryside of Idlib last January, we came across a crumbling wall with hideous graffiti on it, a remnant of those who were here just a few weeks ago. In uneven, scrawled letters it read: "Assad or we burn down the country!" Then, a few meters ahead stood the police station of the town, freshly painted. Atop its gate, in professional print, appeared the words: "The police and people together for the service of our country."

I had to stop and look back at the crumbling wall and stare again at the writing of the newly cleaned-up building. It was evident that something fresh and new was aching to sprout in Syria, but against extremely difficult odds, while something dark and dated was receding but being maintained with great support and force.

We were a small group of friends from various Syrian backgrounds. Some came to bring aid and baby milk. Others, like me, wanted to witness the reality on the ground. We met with members of the newly formed local councils in the areas we visited. The local councils are new administrative bodies formed by the locals to run civic functions in liberated areas, and are different from the Local Coordination

Committees in Syria (LCC). In one town, two of the elected members were women who came to the gathering held at the house of one of the local leaders of the Free Syrian Army during that cold January night. The women were forceful in voicing their frustrations—lack of bread, lack of educational materials. Not to mention the issues of safety and stress from trying to send their children to school amidst sporadic bombing and shelling.

These were the realities and these were the people trying to organize themselves and run their daily lives while on disconnected islands.

There were many inspiring stories of resilience and survival. The elderly woman, at whose house we stayed said, *"Ya binti, heik ahssan."* Meaning, "My daughter, it's better like this." "We live in liberty and peace, or we die if we get shelled," she said. "I prefer this existence than living in constant fear and stress while the tanks are pointing to my kitchen window." At night she apologized for the bullet hole in the room where we were to sleep. Yet she and her family were the ones who lived with this. The morale of the adults was high, but the faces of the children seemed frozen: their vacant and mournful stares will forever haunt me.

The Syrian people have been doubly hijacked. First when Hafez al Assad, Bashar's father, came to power through a coup d'état in 1970. Then Syrians, caught up in the hope and promise of the Arab Spring, attempted to free themselves from the reign of Bashar al Assad and began their revolution in March 2011, only to find themselves hijacked again by the interests of regional and international powers.

This is what frustrates many of Syria's civic activists. They say their revolution has been taken away.

Mufid[28] is from Daraya, a suburb of Damascus. He has been part of a small nonviolent group since his youth, long before the revolution began in Syria, and has been imprisoned more than once, along with his friends, for their civic activities: cleaning up the neighbourhood, anti-smoking campaigns, creating small libraries. He is an engineer who has a registered patent but discovered, despite his commitment to nonviolent struggle, that he was not willing to leave his community, even when the revolution armed.

He believes that people like him could still make an impact. Even though he is one of the founders of the local council, he is frustrated by the challenges surrounding the Syrian dream for democracy. Turning to armed struggle comes with its price, he says. For him, it is the nature of the beast. "When arms entered the Syrian revolution, and it was a result of the tyranny of the regime and its brutal way of dealing with it, in that moment the leadership of the revolution started leaving the hands of its makers and moving to external powers who supply and bring in arms."

Mufid stresses the importance of holding steadfast to the initial demands of the people to secure a peaceful future in Syria. He is concerned about the escalation in the sectarian tone and actions of the allies of the regime, "especially after the audacious interference in Syria by Iran and Hizbullah." He observes, "I don't see any solution except in what we proposed from the first day of the revolution: A Syrian republic based on equality in citizenship, democratic rule of law, and respect for human rights and for religious and political pluralism."

One of the activists we met while travelling inside was Nicola, a filmmaker from the Christian community in Damascus. He also worked in the theater and was active in the socialist movement before the revolution. Soft-spoken and contemplative, he always gave us astute observations as he was now living in the north and moving between the various liberated areas. He explained the rise of Islamism in the country as being more of a reaction to the constant provocations of the Assad regime and a way of reclaiming an identity under constant siege. Homam Hadad, a young Alawite journalist who left Syria a few months ago and is now working with Syrians in Europe and Turkey, has similar views to Nicola. "The more sectarian side is the regime with no competition, whereas the sectarianism in the revolution is a reaction to a large extent. . . . However, if this continues, sectarianism would deepen in the Syrian mind. But I still can't blame the revolution for sectarianism."

With millions on the streets making their demands, the Syrian regime pushed for a three-layered strategy. First, provoking people to take up arms, where the regime would have the upper hand. Second, orchestrating massive media and e-mail campaigns stressing the threat of Islamic radicalism—and also releasing radicals from prison and hunting down nonviolent and civil right activists. Third, stoking sectarian tensions, even creating them where they did not exist, which has pushed the conflict onto the regional level.

The regime succeeded with these three strategies while failing to achieve its primary goal—crushing the revolution. Yet, Syria is now a country in which the consequences of these three strategies are unfolding with a regime that is also losing control. Many of the civic activists believe the conflict became stalemated when the revolution turned to armed struggle, and think the increasingly Islamized image of the rebellion has served to bolster the regime's propaganda.

Nicola, however, says that this is not just a Syrian crisis, but an international one, given the regional implications of this revolution. Many of the activists point to the failure of dated paradigms of securing strategic interests at the expense of what matters most—namely our very humanity. Eyad from Saraqib, a town near Aleppo, and part of a group of local artists who have been creating murals on the walls of Saraqib, was recently propelled several meters in the air when his workplace was bombed by a MIG26.

Eyad does not feel the solution is complicated. For him, the complexity lies in the international context. "The solution to our complicated context is extremely simple. But the international community is unanimously dealing with us on the basis of securing their own interests."

Hadad also shared his frustrations of a revolution being hijacked. "I feel we have lost our national autonomy and so the stopping of bloodshed is no longer in our hands," he says, "The solution would be by an international decision, unfortunately."

"But," he's quick to add, "I still hope that Syrians will achieve victory through their own internal strength, despite all the odds."

Rasha Qass Yousef is an Assyrian from the north who completed a B.A. in English Literature at the University of Damascus before the revolution. She is currently working in Turkey with an NGO. She also says there has to be political will at the international level to create a collective agreement for a solution that would impose a ceasefire and create a context that would lead to changing the presidential election laws, release all political prisons and set up internationally monitored elections. "But I still don't know how to find a framework to enforce these things," she admits. "For example, the ceasefire—how can we really make it happen by both sides?"

Nicola has thought about this in more detail and believes there can be Syrian solutions. "There is already contact and communication between units of the Syrian regime army and the Free Syrian Army (FSA), especially when it comes to local arrangements for a ceasefire and exchange of captives," he explains. "This could be expanded into a larger circle to cover all of Syria if there is political coordination behind it." He cites the earlier examples of the way many communities—both pro-revolution and pro-Assad—used to send representatives to each other to maintain peace and reconciliation in certain contact areas and how these practices were weakened when the revolution armed.

Emad Alabbar, based in France, is also originally from Daraya and is actively involved in writing and publishing in the Syrian nonviolent movement. His cousin, Giyath Matar, became a national icon and a symbol for the nonviolent movement when he died under torture in prison in September 2011. Despite his personal losses, Alabbar maintains that the solution lies in a peaceful transition.

Yet he also feels that Syrians have lost the momentum of their revolution, with so many regional powers getting involved. He thus recommends a more robust international intervention. "We have as Syrians to realize that accepting gradual solutions is much less costly than continuing this inferno at whose end we may no longer find any of our initial demands." He suggests the formation of a political team that would turn the Syrian issue into a global one through awareness-raising media campaigns that would involve global civil society. "This would create global pressure," he says. "These organizations can remind the international community of their 'responsibility to protect.'"

Alabbar says there should be serious international pressure now, considering that many powers are already involved. Alabbar realizes the implications of such a proposal. "The international community has to intervene to impose a political settlement," he says, "and the Syrians have to realize the consequent compromises might be quiet unfair, but we also have to realize that the alternative is much worse."

Aside from the many international plans and projects for a post-Assad transition designed by Syrians,

including The Day After Project[29] in which I participate, there is considerable evidence on the ground in
Syria of strong civic ideas among ordinary Syrians.
However, they will need the right political environment and assistance to continue the work already
started. This is why a political solution to the crisis
should ensure the continuity of these grassroots and
organic formations. Doing so will allow a transitional
peace plan to be more effective.

Hadad, who has been working with activists on
the Turkish borderlands, says that they are becoming
increasingly critical of armed resistance. "What stands
out," he says, "is that the civil democratic movement
is continuing and critical, rational voices are gaining
strength and clarity among the youth. They have
gained experience on the ground, which the official
opposition [abroad] lacks because of their distance
from the realities here."

Alabbar believes that Syrians today would accept the comprise of an imposed political settlement,
however painful it may be, especially if Syrians realize

such a solution would allow them to accomplish their initial goals more than the path of armed struggle has done or would do if continued. "They will realize also," he explains, "that the revolution does not stop at a specific point and it is not merely to bring down the regime."

Nicola, on the other hand, has specific suggestions to create a Syrian-based solution with some minimal support from the international community. He says that finding a third party within Syria to negotiate between the Syrian regime and the revolutionaries would help navigate the Syrians beyond the current stalemate. "An entity like the National Coordinating Committee," he explains, "even though they are not much liked by the revolutionaries, have their own guys on the ground and are constantly making statements about their willingness to negotiate with the regime." This would "keep the solution inclusively Syrian and on Syrian terms."

"I have friends who are willing to risk their lives to engage in such solutions and negotiations if it would stop the bloodshed," he adds. He also suggests that if there is some measure of safety and immunity given to such an entity by the international community, this undertaking would place real pressure on the regime.

We know what would happen if there were a minimal level of safety from regime shelling and brutality. It is the hushed option. If Syrians had a minimal measure of security they would be on the streets again demanding a peaceful regime change. For over six months Syrians did just that. They remained nonviolent despite the brutal and inhuman provocations of the regime.

Mirna is a computer engineer from the Southern city of Daraa. She explains how activists get frustrated when Syria is compared to Iraq. "They say Iraq was an egg that was crushed, but Syria is a chick trying to break its shell from within and is in need of protection." For the activists, she says, revolution and invasion are two different realities with different implications.

Syrians are anxiously anticipating a new dawn, but many factors and powers are stretching the dark night of their suffering. If all the options that could save Syria are ignored and the country is abandoned to the chaos of sectarian provocations, regional tensions, and international interests, Syria will be yet another mirror of the failure of the international order.

The cover of the February 23, 2013 edition of *The Economist* bore the headline "Syria: The Death of a Country." A more apt headline would have been "The Betrayal of a Country."

Syria Is Not a Problem from Hell—But If We Don't Act Quickly, It Will Be

ForeignPolicy.com, May 31, 2012

Anne-Marie Slaughter

NOTHING TO BE DONE. IT'S IMPOSSIBLE. Stalemate at the United Nations.

These are the mantras that continue to accompany ever more violent and wrenching pictures of massacres and daily killings in Syria. The country has been "sliding toward civil war" for months now without any meaningful change in the international response. The Russian government originally seems to have calculated that President Bashar al-Assad could crush the opposition the way Vladimir Putin crushed the uprising in Chechnya, but that degree of brutality would have brought international intervention for sure. The "Annan Plan" is becoming a synonym for hypocrisy and inaction. The Friends of Syria diplomatic strategy of choking the Syrian economy ever tighter is paying off in food shortages and rising prices, but has offered no evidence that the Sunni business class has the will or the means to effect a coup. And the Alawites appear to be closing ranks; indeed, massacres like the May 25, 2012, slaughter in al-Houla guarantee an increasingly bloody retribution if and when the tide finally turns.

I say "if" and not just "when" because Lebanon teaches us that an even more violent and chaotic version of the present conflict can endure for years, but with the added dimension of growing radicalization of many opposition forces and the provision of a new cause and new territory for al Qaeda-linked or inspired insurgents from Iraq, Yemen, and even Pakistan. These elements truly are the "foreign terrorists" Assad inveighs against; their presence and their IED and car-bomb tactics will solidify support for Assad in Damascus and Aleppo and drive Syria's Alawites ever more deeply into the arms of Iran. At the same time, trouble spills over into Lebanon as Syrian government troops chase Free Syrian Army (FSA) forces across the border, a scenario that could be replicated in Jordan and Turkey. All the while, Syria's Kurds are freer to unite with their Iraqi cousins, with dreams of an expanded Kurdish autonomous zone that is a nightmare for the Turkish government. Add chemical weapons, and the designs of Iran, Israel, Qatar, Russia, and Saudi Arabia into the mix and long-term destabilization of the region's security and economy looms.

An alternative exists, one that grows clearer and nearer every day. Three months ago, I proposed in the *New York Times* that the Arab League and Turkey, backed by NATO members, should provide a limited number of specialized anti-tank and anti-mortar weapons to Syrian towns willing to declare "no kill zones"—call them NKZs—in their towns, meaning no attacks by the Syrian army, sectarian *shabbiha* militias, the FSA, or anyone else. Public safety, including for peaceful protesters, would be paramount. I suggested the United States provide communications and intelligence to enable the town authorities and any members of any military willing to enforce the NKZ to allow them to track the movements of Syrian government troops. And I suggested that drones from Jordan, Saudi Arabia, Turkey, and the United States could fire on Syrian government tanks approaching NKZs.[30]

This proposal was widely met with derision, particularly in the security community. But three months later, the United States has announced that it is providing intelligence and communication support to the FSA and openly countenancing the provision of arms by Qatar and Saudi Arabia. Near the Jordan-Syria border, the U.S. military has just finished a massive military exercise with Jordan and 18 other countries. Ambassador Susan Rice told CNN's Wolf Blitzer Wednesday night that as a last resort "we," presumably meaning the Friends of Syria, must "look at options outside the U.N." Robert Baer, who spent more than two decades as a CIA case officer in the Middle East, said on another CNN program that it would be possible to use drones to take out tanks in Syria. And the *Times* of London came out in support of no-kill zones on its editorial page.

What is still missing is a plan. It is time to stand neither for the Syrian opposition nor against the Syrian government but against killing by either side. To tell any Syrian local officials willing to stand against killing—whether a Local Coordination Committee or simply a municipal government—that they will receive weapons and air support against tanks, support that will be withdrawn if killing begins or continues, by anyone. All citizens of such towns should be instructed to photograph violence by anyone against anyone and upload it to a central website maintained by the U.N. or by the Friends of Syria, so that they become peace monitors.

Legally, the Friends of Syria can proceed without the U.N. Security Council's approval if the Arab League is willing to declare a threat to regional peace and security resulting from the ongoing violence in Syria. Given the current refugee situation and the clear potential for destabilization of neighboring countries, the league would be amply justified in doing so. Arab states are also entitled to ask for assistance from Turkey and any other countries. NATO could make the same move at Turkey's request, but need not do so for individual NATO members to assist the Arab League. International lawyers will debate the point, but Chapter VIII of the U.N. Charter governing regional arrangements arguably allows such action as long as the Arab League informs the Security Council of the measures it is taking for the maintenance of international peace and security.

Baer, the former CIA officer, also said on CNN that it was quite possible that the international community would not intervene in Syria until the level of killing reached Rwandan proportions. That is a horrific message to send both to the Syrian people and the Syrian government, not to mention similarly brutal governments around the world. Surely mass murder in the tens of thousands is enough for action, on both moral and strategic grounds.

Many if not most readers will have objections to the plan proposed here. To them, I say: Either accept the status quo and recognize how much worse it is likely to get, or propose a plan of your own.

Supporting Unarmed Civil Insurrection in Syria

ForeignPolicy.com, "Supporting non-violence in Syria,"
December 20, 2012

Stephen Zunes

THE WORSENING VIOLENCE AND REPRESSION in Syria have left many analysts and policymakers in the United States and other western countries scrambling to think of ways our governments could help end the bloodshed and support those seeking to dislodge the Assad regime. The desperate desire to "do something" has led a growing number of people to advocate for increased military aid to armed insurgents or even direct military intervention.

While understandable, to support the armed opposition would likely exacerbate the Syrian people's suffering and appear to validate the tragic miscalculation by parts of the Syrian opposition to supplant their bold and impressive nonviolent civil insurrection with an armed insurgency.

The Assad regime proved itself to be utterly ruthless in its suppression of the nonviolent pro-democracy struggle in 2011. However, it is important to stress that this ruthlessness was not the primary reason the movement failed to generate sufficient momentum to oust Bashar al-Assad.

From apartheid South Africa to Suharto's Indonesia to Pinochet's Chile, extremely repressive regimes have been brought down through largely nonviolent civil insurrections. In some cases, as with Marcos in the Philippines, Honnecker in East Germany, and Ben Ali in Tunisia, dictators have ordered their troops to fire into crowds of many thousands of people, only to have their soldiers refuse. In some other countries, such as Iran under the Shah and Mali under General Toure, many hundreds of nonviolent protesters were gunned down, but rather than cower the opposition into submission, they returned in even larger numbers and eventually forced these dictators to step down.

Historically, when a nonviolent movement shifts to violence, it is a result of frustration, anger, or the feeling of hopelessness. Rarely is it done as a clear strategic choice. Indeed, if the opposition movement were organizing its resistance in a strategic way, with a logical sequencing of tactics and a familiarity with the history and dynamics of popular unarmed civil insurrection, they would recognize that it is usually a devastating mistake to shift to violence. Rather than hasten the downfall of the dictator, successful armed revolutions have historically taken more than eight years to defeat a regime, while unarmed civil insurrections have averaged around two years before victory. Unfortunately, the fragmentation of Syrian civil society combined with the hardness of the security apparatus has made it challenging to maintain a resilient movement. Whether a movement is violent or nonviolent, improvisation is not enough when dealing with a regime that readily instills fears as in Syria.

Indeed, the failure of the opposition movement to overthrow the regime in its initial months, when it was primarily nonviolent, does not prove that nonviolence "doesn't work" any more than the failure of a violent movement to overthrow a regime subsequently proves that violence "doesn't work." Whether or not a movement is primarily violent or nonviolent, what is important is whether it employs strategies and tactics that can maximize its chances of success.

Another factor is that, unlike the Ben Ali regime in Tunisia, the Mubarak regime in Egypt, the Saleh regime in Yemen, or the Qaddafi regime in Libya, Syria is not a case of a regime whose power rests in the hands of a single dictator and the relatively small segment of the population that benefits from their association with the dictator. The Syrian regime still has a social base. A fairly large minority of Syrians—consisting of Alawites, Christians and members of other minority communities, Baath Party loyalists and government employees, the professional armed forces and security services, and the (largely Sunni) crony capitalist class that the regime has nurtured—still cling to the regime. There are certainly dissidents and "latent double thinkers" within all of these sectors. Yet regime loyalists are a large enough segment of the population so that no struggle—whether violent or nonviolent—will win without cascading defections.

The Baath Party has ruled Syria for most of the past 50 years, before even the 30-year reign of Assad's father. Military officers and party apparatchiks have developed their own power base. Dictatorships that rest primarily on the power of just one man are generally more vulnerable in the face of popular revolt than are oligarchical systems in which a broader network of elite interests has a stake in the system. Just as the oligarchy which ruled El Salvador in the 1980s proved to be far more resistant to overthrow by a popular armed revolution than the singular rule of Anastasia Somoza in neighboring Nicaragua, it is not surprising that Syria's ruling group has been more resilient relative to the personalist dictatorships toppled in the wave of largely nonviolent insurrections in neighboring Arab countries which climaxed last year.

What this means is that, whatever the method of struggle in Syria, it was always likely to have been a protracted one. Armed struggle is not a quick fix. Whether a popular struggle against an autocratic regime succeeds depends not on the popularity of the cause or even the repression of state security forces, but on whether those engaged in resistance understand the basis of the real power of the regime and develop a strategy that can neutralize its strengths and exploit its vulnerabilities.

Nonviolent struggle, like armed struggle, will succeed only if the resistance uses effective strategies and tactics. A guerrilla army cannot expect instant success through a frontal assault on the capital. They know they need to initially engage in small low-risk operations, such as hit and run attacks, and take the time to mobilize their base in peripheral areas before they have a chance of defeating the well-armed military forces of the state. Similarly, it may not make sense for a nonviolent movement to rely primarily on the tactic of massive street demonstrations in the early phases of a movement, but diversify their tactics, understand and apply their own strengths, and exploit opportunities to mobilize support and increase the pressure on the regime.

There is little question that the Assad regime feared the ability of the nonviolent opposition to neutralize the power of the state through the power of civil resistance more than it has armed groups that are attacking state power where it is strongest— through the force of arms. They recognized that an armed resistance would reinforce the regime's unity and divide the opposition. That is why the regime has so consistently tried to provoke the pro-democracy forces into violence. It claimed that the opposition was composed of terrorists and armed thugs even during the early months of the struggle, when it was almost completely nonviolent, recognizing that the Syrian people were far more likely to support a regime challenged by an armed insurgency than through a largely nonviolent civil insurrection.

Encouraging defections from the government's side is essential. Defections by security forces—critically important in ousting a military-backed regime—are far more likely when they are ordered to gun down unarmed protesters than when they are being shot at. Defection, however, is rarely a physical act of soldiers spontaneously throwing down their arms, crossing the battlefield and joining the other side. Not everyone can do that. Sometimes defections come in the form of bureaucrats or officers degrading the effectiveness of the regime through quiet acts of noncooperation, such as failing to carry our orders, causing key paperwork to disappear, deleting computer files, or leaking information to the other side.

In turning to armed resistance, what was once a political struggle becomes an existential struggle, and therefore more difficult to win people to your side. One's loyalty to the regime may depend in large part on how they perceive the alternative. They need to decide whether the goal of the opposition is to create an inclusive Syria in which all political factions and sectarian communities will play a part or whether they instead simply seek to destroy their perceived opponents. The chances of bringing down Assad will be greatly enhanced if Syrians are forced to choose not between two savage forces, but between a repressive regime and more inclusive representative movement.

An unarmed civil insurrection which resists the temptation to fight back with violence gives those who may be in a position to defect real hope that they would be welcomed in joining the opposition in building a more democratic and pluralistic system in which they could have a part. By contrast, facing an armed movement—particularly one which has engaged in acts of terrorism and targets minority communities and other alleged supporters of the government—gives rise to fears that they will be persecuted or even executed if the opposition wins, and will therefore fight even harder. In short, armed struggle hardens rather than weakens the resolve and unity of repressive regimes.

The most critical limitation of armed struggle is that its occurrence can significantly decrease the number of participants in a movement or popular opposition since most citizens are unwilling to put their own lives at risk. Another significant limitation is that armed struggle plays to the strength of an authoritarian regime, which commands the arena of military force. When the armed wing of the insurgency initially came to predominate in Syria toward the end of 2011, there was still a fair amount of nonviolent resistance as well. As late as April 12, the initial day of the United Nations-brokered cease-fire (and the only day it effectively held), the largest demonstrations since before the launch of the armed struggle happened. However, armed opposition elements feared the cease-fire might simply give the regime time to stall, enact some reforms, and reinforce its standing, and immediately resume fighting. This gave the regime the excuse to engage in some of the worst massacres to date and the cease-fire completely collapsed.

When the armed resistance escalated dramatically in 2012 after the failure of the cease-fire late in the spring and into the summer, it proved deleterious to the civil insurrection and dramatically increased the death toll. From May to August, the monthly death toll rose from 1322 to 5039 while the number of Friday demonstrations declined from 834 to 355. Subsequently, the weekly total has been well under 300. Indeed, despite claiming to defend the civilian population from the regime's armed forces, they have only succeeded in fearfully increasing the civilian death toll.

A large fraction of former nonviolent protesters have since embraced the armed struggle and, given the horrific repression the opposition has faced from the brutal regime, it would be difficult for observers in the West to pass moral judgment on individuals who have made that choice. However, for those of us who want to see the Assad regime replaced with a true democratic government, there are plenty of reasons to question that choice on strategic grounds.

And there are many Syrians still involved in the nonviolent struggle who agree.

According to pro-democracy activist Haythan Manna, the turn to armed struggle has resulted in the fragmentation of opposition groups and has served to "undermine the broad popular support necessary to transform the uprising into a democratic revolution. It made the integration of competing demands—rural v. urban, secular v. Islamist, old opposition v. revolutionary youth—much more difficult." He also noted how the militarization of the resistance has "led to a decline in the mobilization of large segments of the population, especially amongst minorities and those living in the big cities, and in the activists' peaceful civil movement." He also notes how the armed struggle has increased the influence of hardline Islamists, noting, "The political discourse has become sectarian; there has been a Salafization of religiously conservative sectors."

Another problem with armed struggle historically is that it can lead what were independent indigenous movements to become dependent upon foreign powers who supply them with arms, as happened to various popular left-wing nationalist movements in the Global South during the Cold War which ended up embracing Soviet-style Communism and adopting Moscow's foreign policy prerogatives. While the initial pro-democracy movement explicitly rejected sectarianism, the Wahhabi-led regimes of Saudi Arabia and Qatar saw the challenge to Assad, an Alawite, as a means of breaking the so-called "Shiite crescent" stretching from Iran through Iraq to southern Lebanon. These autocratic Sunni monarchies clearly do not have a democratic agenda, yet—thanks to the armed struggle—they have developed significant influence. Gulf-based networks like Wisal and Safa pushed the Salafi line that the Syrian revolution should be seen not as a diverse pro-democracy struggle, but part of a global "jihad."

As a result of all this, there are serious questions as to whether it is appropriate for the United States and other foreign powers to support the armed resistance. Providing military support to a disorganized and fragmented armed resistance movement means more people getting killed; it does not necessarily create a disciplined fighting force capable of defeating a well-armed regime, much less establishing a stable democratic order. Even more problematic would be direct military intervention.

Furthermore, given that there are now heavily-armed Islamist extremists and others involved in the resistance, there is no guarantee that Assad's overthrow would actually bring peace. U.S. occupation forces in Iraq soon found themselves caught in the middle of a bloody sectarian conflict and quickly learned that some of Saddam's biggest foes were also quite willing to turn their guns on the "foreign infidels."

In order for an unarmed civil insurrection to succeed, it is necessary to build a coalition representing broad segments of society, requiring the kind of compromise and cooperation which can provide the basis for a pluralist democratic order in the future. As a result, the majority of countries in which dictatorships are overthrown by nonviolent insurrections are able to establish stable democratic institutions and processes within a few years. By contrast, since armed struggles are centered on an elite vanguard with a strict military hierarchy and martial values, these patterns of leadership often continue once rebel military commanders become the new political leaders. Indeed, history has shown that dictatorships overthrown by armed revolutions are far more likely to become new dictatorships. Furthermore, there is also a high correlation with the method of struggle and political stability: countries in which the old regime was toppled through armed struggle are far more likely to experience civil war, coups d'état, and dangerous political volatility subsequently. This may be particularly true in light of the potentially explosive ethnic and sectarian mosaic of Syria.

In sum, opposition to U.S. support for the armed resistance in Syria has nothing to do with indifference, isolationism, or pacifism. Nor is it indicative of being any less horrified by the suffering of the Syrian people or any less desirous of the overthrow of Assad's brutal regime. With so much at stake, however, it is critical to not allow the understandably strong emotional reaction to the ongoing horror or a romanticized attachment to armed revolution serve as a substitute for strategic thinking in our support for and solidarity with the Syrian struggle for freedom.

A Syrian Case for Humanitarian Intervention
Radwan Ziadeh

SINCE THE STRUGGLE FOR FREEDOM AND democracy in Syria began in March 2011, Syrian security forces and the Syrian army have killed at least 80,000 people and laid complete waste to the country. More than 1.5 million refugees have fled to Turkey, Jordan, Lebanon, and Iraq, and 5 million Syrians have been forced to abandon their homes due to the violence. According to reports issued by the United Nations and international human rights organizations, Syrian government forces have routinely bombarded densely populated civilian areas with artillery, deployed snipers and helicopters in urban areas, and tortured detained protestors and human rights activists. All of these acts are considered Crimes Against Humanity as defined by the Rome Statute that established the International Criminal Court (ICC) in 2002.

After similar war crimes and crimes against humanity took place in the former Yugoslavia and Rwanda, the General Assembly of the United Nations established the "Responsibility to Protect" or R2P in 2005. R2P argues that a state surrenders its sovereignty when it commits acts of genocide, ethnic cleansing, war crimes, or crimes against humanity on its territory. As a member of the United Nations, Syria is committed to this duty to protect its citizens from these crimes. When the Syrian government launches constant indiscriminate attacks against unarmed civilians, it is clearly failing to comply with this principle, thereby transferring the responsibility to protect unarmed Syrian citizens directly to the international community.

In a United Nations report published in 2009, UN Secretary-General Ban Ki-moon characterized the three pillars underpinning the R2P principle: First, each state has a permanent responsibility to protect its population from genocide, war crimes, ethnic cleansing and crimes against humanity, and all that incites those crimes. Second, it is the responsibility of the international community to provide assistance to states to comply with the obligations contained in the first point. Third, if the state has clearly failed to protect its people, the international community must respond to the situation decisively and in a timely manner, based on Chapters VI, VII, and VIII of the U.N. Charter, and to take appropriate measures, peaceful or otherwise. In addition, in emergency situations, international alliances can be established to stop gross violations of international law, even without prior approval of the Security Council.

Despite the fact that Syria is a clear-cut candidate for the application of R2P, the international community has essentially abandoned Syrians to die at the hands of their government. The United States, which called for the removal of President Bashar al-Assad in 2011, has thus far utterly failed at following up its words with decisive action. And, for more than a year, the U.N. Security Council has proven itself incapable of adopting a resolution regarding Syria, not even to condemn the atrocities perpetrated by the Syrian regime, thanks to Russian veto power.

The Friends of Syria group, which was established specifically for the sake of creating a venue outside of the United Nations in which an international coalition could begin considering actions that would protect the lives of Syrian civilians, has offered only words of sympathy and empty promises to the Syrian people. Syrians have learned not to expect much from the international community after many conferences concluded without adopting any meaningful decisions. They consider these gatherings, like Friends of Syria meetings, as nothing more than opportunities for giving sympathetic speeches.

The United States should work with E.U. allies to achieve the main goals for which the Friends of Syria group was initially established: to conduct an international humanitarian intervention to protect Syrian civilians.

In ideal circumstances, a humanitarian intervention—the use of force for humanitarian means—would be instituted via the U.N. Security Council. Unfortunately, Russian veto power stands in the way of this option. Russia remains unwilling to grant Western powers additional abilities to check the power of regimes, no matter how evil, in its backyard. But precedent for conducting a humanitarian intervention outside the auspices of the Security Council already exists—Western allies have previously enforced no-fly zones over Iraq without the explicit approval of the Security Council. Some form of intervention could absolutely be instituted either under the umbrella of the Friends of Syria group or some other international coalition.

But what would such an intervention look like? A number of options remain available to the international community, including: targeted airstrikes, a no-fly zone, a buffer zone, a humanitarian zone, the training of opposition forces, and the arming of opposition forces. Both Western powers and regional allies are already engaging in the latter two options. Media reports clearly show that the United States has approved training programs for Free Syrian Army soldiers in Jordan and given the green light for the distribution of Croatian arms (paid for and transported by Gulf partners) to rebel battalions operating under the command structure of the Supreme Military Council. Unfortunately these steps are being implemented in such a limited fashion that they have yet to yield particularly tangible results inside Syria itself. In fact, without greater commitment to intervention, it seems likely that current activities will only serve to prolong the violence, which, with hundreds killed every day, is already at unacceptable levels.

A humanitarian zone, or humanitarian corridor, could be implemented along the Turkish and Jordanian borders. The purpose of such a zone would be explicitly to protect Syrian civilians from the imminent and constant threat that the Syrian army and air force pose to them. Such a zone is difficult to establish without a large number of ground troops, however. 13,000 soldiers were needed to create a 10,000 square kilometer safe zone in Iraq in 1991. And, in reality, neither the Syrian opposition nor the international community are particularly enthused by the idea of "boots on the ground" in Syria.

The option of creating a buffer zone presents similar difficulties. Buffer zones, which are used to separate two warring parties, require peacekeeping forces and the consent of both sides of a conflict. Though a buffer zone would certainly have the effect of protecting civilians over a limited territory, the intervention would be limited in its scope and results and require soldiers provided by other countries, a scenario both unlikely and unwanted by the international community and most members of the Syrian opposition.

The creation of a no-fly zone, on the other hand, would not require the occupation of Syria by foreign soldiers. It would, however, require a significant investment of military hardware by the implementing nation or coalition. A no-fly zone would directly aid in civilian protection by preventing the aerial bombardment of civilian populations. But, it would require the active patrol of Syrian airspace. Thus far, members of the international community have been unwilling to make the investment required to enforce such a no-fly zone. This is why some have suggested the creation of a de facto no-fly zone through the arming of opposition forces with man portable air defense systems (MANPADS). The opposition has in fact obtained a small number of these weapons, and they have been somewhat effective, but many more weapons systems would be needed before making a tangible effect on the levels of violence propagated by the regime against Syrian civilians. And, in reaction to the opposition's procurement of MANPADS, the Syrian government quickly changed its tactics. Syria now uses long-range ballistic missiles to indiscriminately attack areas in which it can no longer utilize its air power.

Targeted air strikes remain the option most likely to erode the Syrian government's ability to commit crimes against humanity. Strategic strikes would eliminate crucial military targets such as regime military, air, and missile assets and could be accomplished with stand-off weaponry—not a single foreign soldier would enter Syrian territory. Such strikes could also hasten the downfall of the regime, but not without risks. There remains a small chance that such overt action would elicit a retaliatory response from Syrian allies.

It is clear that Syria has now reached such a state of violence that some form of international intervention is necessary to bring a swift end to the conflict. With Syrian regime forces committing crimes against humanity daily against Syrian civilians, according to the R2P doctrine, it is the explicit responsibility of the international community to act to prevent these crimes. Although a humanitarian intervention can take many forms, in the case of Syria, an ideal intervention would involve the empowerment of the

Syrian opposition alongside targeted airstrikes against Syrian regime assets and the enforcement of a no-fly zone to prevent the mass murder of the Syrian people. This comprehensive approach would minimize the amount of international investment required while maximizing immediate and tangible results for protecting innocent Syrians.

Syria: The Case for Staggered Decapitation
Tom Farer

BY IMAGINING WHAT THE OBAMA ADMINISTRA-
TION might have done at the first clear signs that
the demand for change in the Arab world had finally
reached Syria and that the Assad regime was determined to drench it with the blood of its bearers we
may clarify what could be done now.

President Obama had in a sense been preparing
for this moment of truth since his inauguration. He
had explicitly embraced the doctrine of "Responsibility to Protect" (R2P) and declared the prevention
of slaughter to be an important U.S. national security interest. He had drawn into the select ranks of

his national security staff powerful advocates of humanitarian intervention, most notable among them Samantha Power, author of the Pulitzer-Prize-winning *"A Problem from Hell": America and the Age of Genocide*, and had created a senior director for humanitarian emergencies.[31] He had commissioned a high-level bi-partisan commission to advise him on measures to prepare the government to help in preventing another Rwanda. And in light of that Commission's Report he had established a bureaucratic mechanism to trigger cabinet-wide consultation among senior officials in the face of an impending threat of mass-killing in another country.

So the table was set. It wanted only an occasion to dine.

Since 1963 the Assads and their allies had ruled Syria under a State of Emergency which, in effect, gave the President carte blanche to arrest, detain, interrogate by means deemed useful and, in effect, punish anyone he or his numberless avatars among the state's robust security forces deemed a threat to the security of the regime, a power it had exercised pitilessly over the ensuing half century. Being a regime born through brute force and dominated by members of a sectarian minority, the Alawites, themselves a mere eleven percent of a population intensely conscious of its ethnic and religious distinctions, suspicion was native to its existence. It perceived any challenge to its domination of Syrian life, however open and peaceful, as a potentially existential threat. In fact, before the spring of 2011, it had not faced serious resistance since the Muslim-Brotherhood-led insurrection of 1979–82, which culminated in the Hama massacre in that final year when the regime launched an air and artillery assault on insurgent-controlled neighborhoods of the northern city of Hama, reducing them to rubble and killing upwards of 30,000 people.

Given the regime's dubious legitimacy, its narrow sectarian base and history of remorseless rule, and given Syria's possession of the same socioeconomic conditions that had galvanized popular uprisings in

Tunisia, Egypt and Libya—peasants hurled by deteriorating conditions in the countryside into slums on the fringes of major cities and a crony semi-capitalism unable to meet the aspirations either of the urbanized poor or the large, educated middle class—Assad's thinly cosmetic response to the initially peaceful protests that spread across the country in March of 2011 coupled with multiplying arrests, disappearances and murders of protestors had to have alerted the White House to the imminence of massacre. It was latent in the fact that merely exemplary arrest, torture and killing were proving insufficient to halt the rising demand for political changes incompatible with totally arbitrary rule by Assad and his cronies. Unlike Ho Chi Minh in 1950s Vietnam or Fidel Castro in 1960s Cuba, neither Assad nor any other Alawite nor close allies in other communities could be confident of winning any kind of electoral process or otherwise retaining autocratic power without continuing recourse to the structures and methods integral to the form of governance the protestors aimed to dismantle.

Consistent with its leader's personality and following its precedents for alert indecision that the Obama administration had established through its behavior at the outset of popular uprisings in Egypt and Libya, President Obama added his voice to the international chorus calling on Bashar al-Assad to lead a process of change or get out of the way. In light of the Assad regime's nature and Syria's circumstances, the call's futility had to be apparent to all who made it. Anyone with even the most modest appreciation of Syrian reality, much less a man as astute and well informed as President Obama, had to know that the rulers of Syria would not take steps threatening an ultimate loss of control unless confronted by external actors conveying the credible threat of immediate and total loss. Absent that threat, experience told Syria's masters that they could kill their way out of this problem just as they had killed their way out of previous ones. At the time of the Hama insurgency, Bashar's uncle, then head of the security services, was quoted as saying that if necessary he was prepared to create a million martyrs to protect the state. In March of 2011 the regime gave no sign that it had become less prepared.[32]

Whatever may be true in other domains, when it comes to delivering regime-decapitating force across international boundaries, the United States is the exceptional nation. But as Iraq had demonstrated, regime replacement demands boots on the ground. They are not logically required when the purpose of force is merely to deter a regime from doing what comes naturally to it, namely, in this case, terrifying its domestic opponents. To be sure, as I conceded above, without the services of terror, the Assad mafiosi could not absolutely dominate the political and economic life of Syria. They could not sustain a regime of what Karl Wittfogel called Oriental despotism. But from the loss of despotic power it did not follow that they would shrivel into political and economic inconsequence and be stripped of the vast assets accumulated through decades of predation.

Like the Sandinistas in Nicaragua following their electoral defeat in 1990, they could conceivably negotiate a transition in which filaments of their influence would wind indefinitely through the armed forces and security services. They would also exercise influence through their wealth and the administrative and managerial expertise acquired over decades of domination. And while they would lose the power simply to plunder national economic assets, like the Communist Party Nomenklaturas in Eastern Europe, after the loss of absolute power they would be well positioned to acquire privatized state assets and in other ways enhance their place in the national economy.

To be sure, the Sandinistas almost certainly had a larger popular base than does the Assad mafia. The former, indistinguishable from the rest of the Nicaraguan population in ethno-religious terms, had, after all, been the spearhead of that rare phenomenon: a cross-class mass uprising against a brutal, long-entrenched dictatorship, and five years later won a partially open election. The Assads seized control of the Syrian state in 1970 after a protracted power struggle with internal rivals, and have never won a single bona fide electoral contest.

But Syria is, after all, a country of multiple minorities, each with its own anxiety about the implications of an empowered Sunni Arab majority. So the Alawite elite could find electoral allies in the wealthy Christian community and among the perpetually dissatisfied Kurds. Moreover, one might add, even some Sunni Arabs had prospered within the Alawite order. Furthermore, Sunni Arabs had urban-rural, class, and secular-Islamist fault-lines. There were, in short, internal contextual features of Syrian society available to make a negotiated opening of the political system less frightening to the Assad clan if and when they were compelled to consider this alternative.

In the Spring of 2011, and still today two bloody years later, Washington had the means to compel, namely through awesome stand-off capacity, to rain carefully discriminating death on the offices of power, notable among them the Presidential Palace and the headquarters of the armed forces and the security services: a visit to Damascus by "Shock and Awe."

Possession of sufficiently lethal means is one condition of successful coercion. An evident will to use them is a second one. The third necessary condition, one intimately related to the second, is a demand that the targeted actor can satisfy at conspicuously less cost than its interlocutor threatens to impose if the demand is not met. In addition to seeking only a structured transition from autocracy rather than the extinction of the autocrats, the US could have helped to satisfy the third condition by agreeing to protect the autocrats from international criminal proceedings and even to safeguard assets in U.S. financial institutions.

Steps to demonstrate seriousness of intent would include the following:

• orchestrating a call from the largest possible set of Arab governments, but particularly from Saudi Arabia and Egypt, to assist the people of Syria by all necessary means to exercise their right to protest peace-fully and to achieve a "representative" government;

• securing, through the efforts of the Saudis and President Morsi of Egypt, fatwas from eminent clerics authorizing non-Muslim states to assist in protecting the Syrian people; noisily ordering the reinforcement of cruise-missile-equipped naval assets in the Mediterranean and deploying existing ones off the Lebanese coast;

• with the agreement of Turkish President Gül and Prime Minister Erdoğan, initiating the deployment in Turkey of Patriot Missile units and attack aircraft;

• a call from President Obama to Vladimir Putin urging a joint initiative to forge a transition to more representative Syrian government, assuring him that the U.S. would not seek to supplant Moscow as Syria's armorer, but also assuring him that, in light of the calls from Arab governments and the fatwas, the U.S. was prepared to use decimating force with or without (if necessary) a Security Council Resolution.

These actions would succeed a call to Assad from Obama himself, clarifying U.S. desires and intentions and expressing his readiness to send his Secretaries of State and Defense to Damascus to discuss how U.S.–Syrian relations could be put on benignly convergent tracks. The moves sketched above would follow on immediately from rejection of Obama's proposal or failure of the proposed meeting in Damascus to end the brutalization of protestors and to catalyze substantial steps toward a broadly representative government.

Would these moves be sufficient to make the U.S. threat credible? Quite possibly not. Reminiscing about a trip to Syria some years earlier, the journalist T.A. Frank, who had previously spent time in China, wrote: "China was a place of cruelty and corruption but also vision, a place where personal greed could coexist with at least some plan for national progress. In Syria . . . the feeling in the air was one of stupid backward-looking repression for no purpose other than to shut everyone up."[33] To get the serious attention of prehensile thugs, you probably need to apply a bat to the side of one of their heads. So yes, we might have had to smash the headquarters of a security service or the armored limousine of a close relative of Bashar with him in it in order to lubricate a serious discourse about the Syrian government's Responsibility to Protect.

As a means to end the slaughter and to force a negotiated transition before Syria becomes Afghanistan in the 1990s, staggered or one might call it sequential decapitation remains the best among various bad options available to the United States, assuming as I do that appeals from the key regional states and the fatwas can be secured. I assume as well that a U.S. appeal to the mafia regime in Moscow for a decisive joint effort to shape a new Syrian regime, one incorporating all sects and militias that are willing to be part of a broadly representative order marked by carefully balanced sectarian power, will fail.

Of course in many if not quite all respects the circumstances for this or any other policy option are far worse now than in March 2011. After the death of 70,000 people (the proportionate equivalent of roughly 12 million dead in the United States) and countless more crippled and disfigured and homeless, a total amnesty for the Assad mafia will be, shall we say, a hard sell even to the most moderate of its opponents. So much blood translates into very personal, very gut-level hatred among the now multiply fractured and armed elements of Syrian society that would need to buy into a settlement that could possibly endure.

In two respects, however, conditions may be more favorable for the option of staggered decapitation. First, Syria no longer registers in the minds of US political elites and opinion-shapers as a primarily humanitarian problem. The dangers stemming from Syria's progressive disintegration into a lawless space relentlessly drawing into itself furious fighters with jihadist and borderless agendas, a scenario dimly if at all perceived two years ago, are now evident. Hence the US domestic political environment for bold action is more promising. Secondly, it must be apparent to the senior members of the Assad mafia that U.S. airpower could break the present military stalemate and open the door to their liquidation.

The table is set. It is past time to dine.

A Humanitarian Strategy Focused on Syrian Civilians

opendemocracy.net, "Bordering on a New World War I," April 27, 2013

Mary Kaldor

"Can I ask you a question?" said the person I was interviewing on a recent trip to southern Turkey. He had owned a water pump store in northern Syria and left with his family because of the constant shelling and bombardment, including the use of white phosphorus. Now he is part of a self-organized Syrian group providing relief to refugees now living in camps in the area and representing their voices. "This is the Holocaust," he said. "This is the First World War. Why is no one in Europe doing anything? Can you explain it?"

It was a question I asked myself repeatedly during

my visit. According to the latest Office of the United Nations High Commissioner for Refugees (UNHCR) figures, there are some 1.3 million Syrian refugees, of which 300,000 are in southern Turkey. The Turkish authorities estimate some 190,000 refugees in camps in southern Turkey and a similar number outside the camps. They expect a million refugees by the end of the year if the situation does not change. Some 70,000 people have been killed. Hundreds of thousands are internally displaced.

The war in Syria began in March 2011 when the regime began shooting at peaceful protestors. After a few months, some Syrians began shooting back. Groups of armed men began to accompany protests to protect them from attacks by regime security forces and pro-regime militias known as *Shabbiha*. Some were defectors from the Syrian army who refused to fire on protestors. That is how the first units of the Free Syrian Army were formed. They were joined by civilians taking up arms to defend their families, ji-hadist groups such as Jabhat Al Nusra, who include both Syrians and foreign jihadists (especially from Iraq), Kurdish groups, and criminals released from gaol by the regime.

The opposition is said to be fragmented since the Free Syrian Army (FSA) consist of independent self-organized brigades alongside these various armed actors. There are also accusations of sectarianism and jihadism. The regime, which relies on terrifying its Alawite base into believing the opposition are Sunni extremists intent on massacring Alawites, has deliberately attempted to foment sectarian violence, making use of the *Shabbiha* to attack Sunni communities. It has also tried to court Kurdish political parties.

There have been sectarian incidents, but the opposition includes all ethnic and religious groups. The western press often wrongly portray Syria in sectarian terms despite the long cosmopolitan tradition in the country. The jihadist Jabhat Al Nusra operates together with the FSA and is gaining adherents, reportedly because it is more efficient as a fighting force and more effective at distributing humanitarian assistance. There are also cases in which Kurdish groups who sided with the regime clashed with the FSA. The opposition outside Syria formed itself into the National Coalition for Syrian Revolutionary and Opposition Forces in November 2012 and includes a range of different groups, many of whom disagree with each other.

The violence has been compounded by the involvement of outside states, including Iran and Russia as well as Hezbollah on the side of the regime, and Saudi Arabia, Qatar, Jordan, Turkey, and Western powers, who back different opposition groups. Syrians speak of a proxy war or a foreign conspiracy.

Outside the main cities of Damascus and Aleppo, where fierce fighting continues, the regime has relinquished control over large parts of the country. Local administrative councils have been established, composed of members of the opposition and prominent local citizens in order to provide services, including water and electricity, food distribution, health and education, garbage collection, and local security. But the regime is pursuing a scorched-earth policy. These areas are subject to constant bombardment, shelling, and missile attacks. Western countries claim to have credible evidence that the nerve gas Sarin has been used. The civilian population and the economic infrastructure are directly targeted. Salaries to government employees have been halted.

There are very few humanitarian agencies operating in the non-government-controlled areas. There are some Islamic agencies—United Moslem, IHH (the Turkish group that organized the Gaza flotilla), and Children in Deen, for example. I met three volunteers from Birmingham who were working with these groups. The only other international NGO working inside the non-government-controlled areas is Médecins Sans Frontières/Doctors Without Borders (MSF). They have organised a field hospital and are trying to organise a programme of measles vaccinations. The head of their emergency unit explained it was a "drop in the ocean." Shockingly, ECHO, the E.U. humanitarian agency, does not provide humanitarian assistance inside Syria and this explains the absence of many European NGOs. There has only been one U.N. convoy when a ceasefire was organized between the government and the FSA.

I met with members of the local administrative council of Raqqa, a town just inside the Turkish border. They had come to Turkey to seek assistance. Their council has representatives from all ethnic and religious groups in the town, including Kurds and Alawites, and also includes a number of women. They also have one member from Al Nusra, but they insisted that Al Nusra must nominate an academic or someone of similar standing. The coordinator of the Council is someone who sees himself as part of the opposition committed to non-violence. They have organized a brigade of the FSA to keep order (the word they used was *amana*, an Arabic word that means safety without any of the connotations relating to security forces of the word "security"). As a result they have avoided the looting and crime that have plagued many other areas.

In addition to the local population, there are 50,000 Internally Displaced Persons (IDPs) in Raqqa. Some 450 people have been killed directly or indirectly as a result of bombardment. The economy has been destroyed. Raqqa depended on agriculture and state salaries. The regime destroyed the electricity infrastructure, which, in turn, has destroyed agriculture, because the irrigation system depends on electricity. State salaries were halted two months ago. There have been some protests recently in favour of going back to the regime. Without outside assistance, we were told, people will be forced to leave the country or to return to the regime.

One person I interviewed argued that the opposition can never win militarily. He argued that the opposition can never match the regime's military force. If attacks on the liberated areas continue, he said, "the revolution is bound to fail." This does not mean the restoration of government control. Rather the prospect is long-term persistent conflict among fragmented fighting groups—a zone of insecurity that links up with other parts of the Middle East and involves a range of global actors. It would be a kind of new World War I.

So why is nothing being done to help people in the non-government-controlled areas? The answer, I think, has to do with the legacy of the War on Terror and the way the situation in Syria has been framed. The war in Syria has been variously described as a revolution, as jihadist/terrorist violence, or as a massive violation of human rights. Western governments interpret the war as a revolution, and their solution is arming the rebels. At the same time they are reluctant to intervene directly because they fear being dragged into a new war after the experience of Iraq and Afghanistan. By the same token, Western leftists fear another imperialistic military intervention. Governments like Russia and China fear terrorism/jihadism/sectarianism and put the emphasis on "order" and "stability," fearing that the same could happen to them if the rebels were allowed to succeed. Iran, Hizbollah, and Saudi Arabia view this as a front in the Sunni/Shi'ia battle for the soul of the Middle East.

What is missing is any serious discussion about the plight of the Syrian people. The polarising effect of the War on Terror meant that the human rights constituency, those who argue for interpreting what is happening as a massive violation of human rights, are increasingly marginalised. The West has argued that the use of chemical weapons is a red line that must not be crossed—a "game changer." If it turns out that this red line has been crossed, then any intervention will be a geopolitical intervention against the Assad regime. The likely response will be to arm the rebels rather to intervene to protect ordinary people. The Western aim would be to help the rebels overthrow the regime because the regime represents a threat to the West as a consequence of its possession and use of weapons of mass destruction.

This is not to oppose the demise of the Assad regime. The point, rather, is that whether or not the regime has used chemical weapons, there should be intervention because of the regime's brutality towards its own people. The priority is to save lives and to reduce the violence. Regime change needs to come about politically, not militarily. In a situation free of fear, Syrians would choose a different way of governing themselves.

What is needed is a humanitarian intervention to protect the Syrian people. How such an intervention is framed is important because it dictates what actually happens. Geopolitical interventions, as in Iraq and Afghanistan, are very different from humanitarian interventions. Humanitarian interventions are, first and foremost, about protecting people—not only in terms of aims but also in terms of methods.

So what would a humanitarian strategy that focused on the civilian population involve? First, there needs to be a focus on empowering and strengthening local administrative councils. They need assistance with the provision of services, including water and electricity, health, education, and local security, as well as the distribution of essentials including food, and help in restarting the economy. There needs to be a substantial increase in humanitarian aid going to the non-government-controlled areas. There also needs to be a much greater international presence, especially if the presence of the U.N. can provide the opportunity for local ceasefires. A demonstration that these areas are viable will help to weaken the regime's position.

Secondly, there needs to be an international buffer zone. Every Syrian with whom I've talked has stressed the need for a No-Fly Zone. With a No-Fly Zone, they contend, the war would have ended already, the liberated administrative councils would have been in a much stronger position and the jihadist groups would have been much weaker. This position was also supported by some Turkish officials with whom I met.

Actually a No-Fly Zone may not be the right term. Much of the damage is done by shelling and missile attacks; indeed close to the Turkish border there are no air attacks because sorties would need to cross into Turkish airspace. What is needed is No

Attacks on Civilians Zones protected by international peacekeepers. This proposal has some similarities to Anne-Marie Slaughter's concept of "No-Kill Zones." But it would be preferable if such zones were internationally protected rather than protected by the FSA, as Slaughter suggests, and if they were negotiated.

The objections to this idea are twofold. First, it is argued that it would be impossible to get international agreement, since Iran, Russia, and China would be opposed. This may well be true, but at least an attempt to negotiate such zones would shift the focus of international negotiations from reaching a top-down political solution to the conflict to addressing the human needs of the Syrian people. Secondly, there are fears that if undertaken by Western countries, it would escalate the proxy international war that is already going on.

In this case, it is important to stress that a protected buffer zone is not the same as intervention on one side or another. It is about reducing violence, not about winning. It is defensive, not offensive. A clear mandate and tight human-rights-based rules of engagement would be critical to underline the nature of such zones. At the very least, efforts to establish such zones would help to shift the international discourse from the issue of whether Assad remains in power or the risks of jihadism and sectarianism to a concern about how to save ordinary Syrians.

How to Ease Syrian Suffering

New York Times, February 8, 2013

Kenneth Roth

THE SYRIAN PEOPLE ARE CAUGHT IN A HORRIBLE downward spiral. The government's slaughter seems only to intensify as President Bashar al-Assad pursues a ruthless strategy of draining the sea to get the fish—attacking civilians so they will flee and leave the armed opposition isolated.

Meanwhile, the sprawling collection of militias that constitute the armed opposition includes some that are themselves torturing and executing prisoners and promoting sectarian strife. While not on a par with the government-directed slaughter, their abuses encourage Syria's minorities to stick with the murderous Assad rather than risk an uncertain future under rebel rule.

The Syrian National Coalition was created to provide a unified command structure that could replace Assad, rein in abusive rebel forces, promote minority rights and pursue a transition that left the state sufficiently intact to avoid a chaotic collapse. Yet the S.N.C. has little clout because it has nothing to offer the people to relieve their suffering.

At the very least, a major influx of humanitarian aid is needed.

So far, most donors have sent aid via operations based in Damascus, meaning little gets to many opposition-held areas of Syria where the suffering is most acute, even when those in need are just across the border from major relief operations in Turkey.

Some humanitarian organizations fear the government will attack them or shut down their Damascus-based operations if they also operate from across Syria's borders. Others are simply following the usual U.N. rules and deferring to the Syrian government.

At least some donors should break from this logic and massively augment growing but wholly inadequate humanitarian aid now crossing from Turkey into Syria through nongovernmental organizations. Aid should be delivered in coordination with rights-respecting elements of the rudimentary civilian governance structures that have been created in opposition-held areas of Syria.

That would help to ease real suffering. It would also enhance the influence of voices in both the international community and Syrian civilian governance structures that are encouraging opposition fighters to respect rights and embrace a vision for the country that includes all Syrians.

Ideally, to maximize effectiveness, cross-border aid should be sent with Damascus's consent or U.N. Security Council approval, but given the intransigence of Assad and his Russian backers, the international community should not wait for permission.

Government forces might still try to bomb the aid, much as they have attacked bakeries and bread lines in northern Syria. But such brazen sabotage of relief efforts would risk retaliatory steps of the sort the international community so far has been unwilling to take.

Even if large-scale cross-border aid proceeds, it is important not to replicate the "well fed dead" phenomenon of Bosnia, where the international community focused on humanitarian aid to civilians rather than ending their slaughter.

The international community, which has a "responsibility to protect" the Syrian people, fears that giving the opposition arms or military support may contribute to a still more repressive future or a sectarian civil war.

Yet the jihadist elements of the opposition have their own networks to obtain arms, reinforcing the international community's propensity to inaction and at the same time allowing Assad to use their power to rally his supporters.

The West has imposed sanctions on the Syrian leadership, but tougher measures—such as worldwide sanctions, a global ban on sending arms to pro-Assad forces or the invocation of the International Criminal Court—have been stymied in the U.N. Security Council by Russia's veto, backed by China.

The international community is wrong to treat Russia's obstruction as reason to give up. More can and should be done, starting with greatly increased cross-border humanitarian aid. And if that aid succeeds in bolstering rights-respecting elements of the armed opposition, it could have important knock-on effects.

A stronger, respected civilian governance structure would have more authority to negotiate an orderly transition in lieu of the chaos and endless civil war that many dread. It could also reduce fears that a successor government might be worse than the current regime.

The carnage in Syria should redouble our determination to end it. A massive cross-border humanitarian operation is feasible, and it could contribute to a virtuous cycle that Syria desperately needs to curb the slaughter of civilians.

KENNETH ROTH   165

*The Last Thing Syrians Need Is
More Arms Going to Either Side*

The Guardian, March 4, 2013

Charles Glass

RUSSIA AND IRAN ARE PROVIDING WEAPONS
and ammunition to Syria's President Assad, while
Saudi Arabia and Qatar deliver arms through Turkey
to his opponents. John Kerry, the U.S. secretary of
state, has just announced that the U.S. is increasing
its non-lethal assistance to the rebels by a further
$60m. Britain is asking the E.U. to lift its embargo
on arms sales to the opposition.

None of this seems designed to end a conflict
that, for a moment, seemed to be heading hesitantly
towards negotiation. Ahmed Moaz al-Khatib, leader
of the Syrian National Coalition, offered last month

to discuss a settlement without demanding Assad's resignation. Assad did not grasp the olive branch, but he did make a proposal of his own in an interview with Hala Jaber in the *Sunday Times*: "We are ready to negotiate with anyone, including militants who surrender their arms."

The militants are no more likely to surrender their weapons, their only means of self-defense, than Assad is to leave office. However, the gap between them was narrowing sufficiently for deft diplomacy to bridge it. Did the powers who have interfered in Syria from the beginning of the uprising in March 2011 get together and demand that their respective clients sit at a negotiating table and hash things out with words rather than bullets? Well, no.

When Assad said that "Britain has played a famously unconstructive role in our region on different issues for decades," he was not far off the mark. A country that, with France, imposed and modified the borders it drew across Ottoman Syria under the Sykes–Picot agreement carries historic baggage. A country that has done nothing since June 1967 to oppose Israel's occupation and annexation of Syria's Golan Heights has a way to go to prove its bona fides to a skeptical Syrian audience. And a country that, from the rebellion's outset, predicted and sought the imminent downfall of the Damascus regime may find it hard to play the role of honest broker.

The person who is attempting to be an honest broker, the United Nations mediator, Lakhdar Brahimi, has no power. All sides in the Syrian war are aware of his impotence, and they ignore his mission knowing that their backers don't back him. Those with power over Syria's fate—the U.S., Russia, Turkey, Iran, Saudi Arabia, Iraq, and Qatar, to name only the most prominent cooks brewing the bloody Syrian stew—are so partisan that they disdain compromise in favor of an immediate if elusive victory for their respective Syrian factions.

Rather than the combatants' benefactors, 24 million Syrians are victims of the escalating arms deliveries to all sides. They face a prolonged war whose casualties will dwarf the estimated 70,000 lives lost to date; more houses destroyed, more refugees; the ruination of their once prosperous economic life; and the shredding of a social fabric that held Syria together for centuries. The U.S., Russia, and the rest seem to say, as secretary of state Madeleine Albright once did about the deaths of half a million Iraqi children due to international sanctions, that "we think the price is worth it." It always is, when someone else pays. Must Syria be destroyed—to recall an American major's observation of the Vietnamese provincial capital of Ben Tre in 1968—in order to save it? Is that what the Syrian people want?

In the interview, Assad said: "You know the crime is not only about the victim and the criminal, but also the accomplice providing support, whether it is moral or ideological support." Britain's foreign secretary, William Hague, declared: "This will go down as one of the most delusional interviews that any national leader has given in modern times." Is it delusional, or should Assad's observation be universalized to apply to his own backers, who implicitly approve his army's actions in the war, as much as to those of the armed opposition? The rebels' own hands—as in any war—are not without blemish. The victims of lethal and non-lethal aid to government and rebels alike are the Syrian people.

Rather than lift the U.S.-European arms embargo on lethal aid, as Britain proposes, why not ask the Russians and Iranians to join it? There is a precedent: the international embargo on arms sales to Israel and its Arab enemies during the war of 1948, when East-West relations were no worse than they are now. As bloody as the 1948 war was, it would have been far worse if the Russians, Americans, French and British had poured in their vast arsenals to Israelis and Arabs alike.

This month marks the second anniversary of Syria's civil war. If the politicians of East and West go on as they are, it will not be the last.

Syria Is Melting
Rafif Jouejati

As horrific as the death toll in Syria is, the impact of Assad's atrocities spreads far wider. Some 22 million Syrians are caught in the crossfire of the regime's desperate attempt to crush all civilian dissent, destroy communities and local councils, and hold on to power in the face of a popular uprising that has turned into an increasingly sophisticated and bearded armed opposition. Foreign jihadists practically found welcome mats at Syria's doorstep as Assad allowed (and encouraged, as some maintain) rampant chaos to spread throughout the country. Meanwhile, Assad and his forces treat medical personnel, teachers, and relief workers as though they pose the same threat as defected soldiers brandishing AK-47s. To this regime, journalists and nonviolent activists are just as threatening as the Free Syrian Army's limited supply of rocket-propelled grenades.

While the carnage has steadily increased in Syria, the West's narrative has not changed: it does not want to arm the opposition for fear that sophisticated weapons that could destabilize the area might end up in the "wrong hands." But those weapons already are, and have long been, in the dreaded "wrong hands": those of the Assad regime, which is doing its best to destabilize the area, and succeeding in doing so. We Syrians know all too well that that the actual "wrong hands" are those of the chemical-weapons-yielding dictatorship that stockpiled them for domestic use. As this conflict wears on, the armed opposition is growing increasingly extremist in the absence of an alternative that would enable average people to defend themselves and their families, one that would enable the defected army to make definitive advances, and allow children to eat and go to school.

Today, Westerners seem to see Syria through an increasingly simplistic and distorting lens. Political analysts and pundits, many of whom appear to have learned all they know about Syria from Wikipedia, glommed onto the terms "civil war" and "sectarian conflict" early on to characterize the situation. They want to view Syria through the same lens with which they view their own societies: African-American, Latino/Hispanic, Caucasian, Asian, and Other. These overly simplified classifications help the West fit people of all backgrounds into neat little boxes. Such intellectual laziness only offers a quick sedative, a little respite from the nagging truth that more than 75,000 people have been killed; that hundreds of men, women, and children across Syria are raped and otherwise sexually tortured every day; or that missiles and cluster bombs have a pesky way of finding their targets at bakery lines. Children are routinely forcibly displaced and frequently targeted by snipers. These atrocities are committed without any specific sectarian agenda in mind; they are committed not because there is an Alawi-Shiite conspiracy or because the Sunnis have been patiently awaiting "their turn." Let us point the finger squarely and unequivocally at the perpetrators: these crimes against humanity are being committed by the Assad regime because the Assad family and security apparatus cannot fathom a country governed by anyone else, let alone free Syrians.

Millions of Syrians in the opposition continue to classify themselves as Syrians—no more, no less. We do not identify ourselves as Christian, Druze, or Ismaili. We are not divided along Alawite-Sunni lines, nor do we want to send minorities to the lions, as it were. We look at our revolution through a very different lens. We fear the regime's sectarian narrative, developed over more than 40 years of tyranny. We don't over-generalize or pigeonhole our compatriots. We make a point to continually reinforce what we have been saying for the past two years: our revolution is not about replacing one dictator with another; our revolution is about freedom, dignity, and democracy for all Syrians. To ignore our voices, or pass them off as naïve, is to ignore the will of most Syrians.

What should be done to stop the human hemorrhaging in Syria? At this point, any sort of forward-moving action in Syria would be a welcome change from the lethargy of empty promises, unfulfilled pledges, and hollow threats. The international community has mostly sat on its hands for the past two years, although it does occasionally (and loudly) condemn violence and proclaim the need for a negotiated political settlement. The United States has repeatedly claimed to support the opposition, and recently sent a new shipment of night-vision goggles to combatants who deal with Scud missiles and whose primary responsibility has become to pull the bodies of children from under the rubble of what used to be apartment buildings. The European Union is divided on what to do in Syria, with some members advocating to arm the opposition in light of the regime's use of chemical weapons; still others continue to quake in fear of the growing number of beards in Syria.

I don't know who coined the phrase, "Count our dead, not our beards," but it has spread throughout activist communities in Syria. And it's absolutely on target. The international community needs to come out of its paralysis and take responsibility for the fact that this humanitarian catastrophe has grown under its watch. The international community, in seeking a negotiated political settlement, must help create a framework in which the killing stops, Syrians are repatriated, and the country can be rebuilt. Failure to do this, and failure to create a mechanism of enforcement that has thus far been missing, only embolden Assad and other tyrants to kill and displace entire populations with impunity. The world's red lines need to be firm and not subject to frequent re-interpretation. As Shadi Hamid has poignantly asked, why is there a red line on chemical weapons but not on 70,000 deaths?[34]

France and the U.K., which might be inclined to arm the more secular elements in the opposition, are waiting for President Obama to stop hiding behind his "leading from behind" policy. The international community can enforce "no kill zones" or no-fly zones to try to stem the river of blood. The international community, particularly the United States, can pressure Iraq into prohibiting Iranian shipments of weapons, and enforce sanctions. The international community can make good on its pledges of more than $1.5 billion in aid that is still not reaching intended recipients. Since the consensus seems to be that a negotiated settlement is what it will take to stop the killing, the international community should negotiate with Assad to establish humanitarian corridors that could be monitored by U.N. personnel with assurances from all armed parties that these monitors will not be attacked. Finally, the E.U., United States, and Arab League can responsibly provide defensive weapons that tip the balance of power both on the ground and in the air, and minimize the risk of having another 100,000 or 1,000,000 dead by this time next year.

And while the international community seeks a negotiated political settlement, we must keep in mind that Assad violated the Arab League initiative of 2011 and the Annan Peace Plan in 2012, then rejected the Brahimi Plan in 2013. If the international community fails to take action before 2014, and continues to let Assad win the game of "chicken" with chemical weapons, the post-World War II vows of "never again" may be reduced to "uh-oh."

Shopping Option C for Syria: Against Arming the Rebels

ForeignPolicy.com, February 14, 2013

Marc Lynch

THE FAILURE OF AMERICAN DIPLOMACY TO end Syria's parade of horrors has rightfully driven the policy community to search for a useful alternative. But arming the rebels was always a classic "Option C." Every bureaucrat knows the trick of offering three options— one to do nothing, one so outlandish that it is easily rejected, and then one that takes the seemingly sensible middle ground, allowing the decision-maker the illusion that they are resolving the problem.

Whether or not Option C has any chance of actually working is almost an afterthought. For an example of how this works, see "the Afghan Surge," which lacked even a plausible theory of how it might work. In Syria, the most likely effect of arming the rebels is simply to set up the president for another decision point six months later as the battle rages and the rebels seem unable to close the deal. And at that point, the president would face an even starker decision: Option A, give up and be tarred forever for cutting and running; Option B, full-scale military intervention, which of course would be rejected; and Option C, escalation through some combination of no-fly zones, a bombing campaign, and safe areas.

When this debate began in earnest one year ago, I predicted that policy would move toward arming the rebels as the easiest way to appear to be "doing something"—even if nobody really believed that it would work. It does not surprise me that Petraeus, Clinton, or Panetta would gravitate toward this option. It surprises me even less to find their preferred policy stance, once it was thwarted, would magically appear in the media. What does surprise me is that the White House managed to cut off this option at the pass.

And don't get it twisted—arming the rebels was "Option C." Sen. John McCain, who has been leading the charge to intervene in Syria, said this summer that arming the rebels was a good step, but "this alone will not be decisive." In fact, he went on to warn that providing weapons "may even just prolong [the conflict]."

McCain's preference was to "make U.S. airpower available, along with that of our allies, as part of an international effort to defend safe areas in Syria and to prevent Assad's forces from harassing [the rebels]." Air power, he believed, could carve out an area inside Syria where the opposition could organize itself, and then use it as a staging area to expand opposition control across the country—much like how the Libyan rebels used the eastern city of Benghazi as their base. The Pentagon, however, had little interest in such a scheme.

Michael Doran and Salman Shaikh have put

forward the strongest case to arm the rebels, which is well worth the read.[35] But even for them, was this really their first, best option—the one they believe will meet with the greatest chance of success? Along with two colleagues from Brookings, this is what Doran and Shaikh had to say 11 months ago:

> While history is replete with states arming opposition groups to weaken their rivals, the precedents for the opposition succeeding quickly in regime change are fewer.... In most cases, supporting an opposition ties down a country's forces and fosters instability but does not topple the regime.... The United States might still arm the opposition even knowing they will probably never have sufficient power, on their own, to dislodge the Assad network. Washington might choose to do so simply in the belief that at least providing an oppressed people with some ability to resist their oppressors is better than doing nothing at all, even if the support provided has little chance of turning defeat into victory.

Alternatively, the United States might calculate that it is still worthwhile to pin down the Assad regime and bleed it, keeping a regional adversary weak, while avoiding the costs of direct intervention.... [T]he U.S. and allied association with the opposition would make it difficult to walk away from them and from Syria if, as is likely, they continue to suffer set-backs or slaughter at the hands of regime forces. Thus pressure to adopt more costly options would grow.

Indeed.

In August 2012, their Brookings colleague Ken Pollack warned, "helping the opposition 'win' might end up looking something like Afghanistan in 2001." Pollack was honest about the implications of a strategy of indirect assistance to the rebels: "[O]ur choice will almost certainly be between picking a winner and leading a multilateral intervention. Chances are we will start with the former, and if that fails to produce results, we will shift to the latter."[36] Indeed.

Those pessimistic conclusions match the academic consensus that "civil wars with outside involvement typically last longer, cause more fatalities,

and are more difficult to resolve through negotiations."[37] This is particularly the case when there are
multiple potential external backers with conflicting
objectives, as is the case in Syria. Hence the constant
refrain that U.S. reticence is allowing Gulf money—
which goes overwhelmingly to Islamist groups—to
carry the day.

It's difficult to produce a single example in modern history of a strategy of arming rebels actually
succeeding. Please, please, don't offer the example of
U.S. support for the Afghan jihad in the 1980s—because I'll just see that and raise you a collapsed state,
warlordism, rise of the Taliban, and al Qaeda. Meanwhile, there are plenty of examples of the overt or
covert provision of arms to a rebel group prolonging
and intensifying conflicts, and lots of cases of rebel
groups happily taking our money and guns to "fight
communists" (or whatever) and then doing whatever
they like with them. That doesn't mean that such a
strategy couldn't work in Syria, but history is most
definitely not on its side.

That was then—what about now? Many very sharp analysts, ranging from Steven Heydemann to Salman Shaikh, argue that with militarization a reality, the United States should manage the process, accelerating the endgame and gaining influence over the Syrian opposition by taking a leading role in directing the flow of arms.[38] As I've pointed out, this case has grown stronger with time: Some of the key reasons for avoiding arming the rebels no longer apply, since the negative effects of militarization have already largely manifested.[39]

Robin Yassin-Kassab may have a case that arming the moderates has never really been tried, but there's no question that arms have flooded in and the Syrian arena has become fully militarized.[40] There's not much of a political process to save: undecided Syrian constituencies have already retreated back into the embrace of the regime, arms are flowing, the men with guns are calling the shots, and a new political economy of insurgency has taken root.

In this context, a coordinated flow of arms is

superior to an uncoordinated flow of arms. But I doubt that an American decision to get into that game would do much good. Offering weapons and money might buy influence in the moment, but they don't buy love or guarantee the alignment of values or priorities. The reporting from inside Syria offers a consistent portrait of emergent warlordism, with local commanders eager to take bids from external patrons. Arming and funding militias basically means renting them until a better offer comes along, as suggested by the endless parade of articles reporting Syrian groups turning to Islamists because they are better financed or better armed.

Sure, the United States could enter this crowded market—but why would anyone expect Washington to dominate it, or to fundamentally change its patterns? It won't make the Islamist groups tied to al Qaeda disappear—they were drawn to the opportunity to wage jihad, and they certainly aren't going to leave just because America decides to muscle onto their turf. It is also not obvious why U.S.-provided weapons would be better or more attractive than Gulf weapons, especially if ours come with human rights guidelines and inconvenient political limitations.

Everyone wants to find a way to end the killing in Syria. But there's very little reason to believe that American arming of the rebels would achieve that goal. President Barack Obama's administration was right to focus instead on sorting out the opposition leadership, and trying to establish it as an effective political umbrella rather than turning on an arms pipeline to the rebels.

That's not to say there isn't more the United States can be doing. I do think the administration missed a major opportunity to rapidly funnel significant humanitarian aid and non-lethal support through the National Coalition it laboriously helped construct, in order to give them something to offer Syrians on the ground. Fixing that should be a priority.

The ever-escalating disaster in Syria cries out for more effective international diplomacy, vastly more humanitarian support for refugees and the displaced, and more work to strengthen the political structures of the opposition. Efforts should be focused on such initiatives, rather than on a poorly conceived Option C which drags the United States deeper into an abyss with no real prospect of victory.

The Price of Inaction in Syria

Spiegel Online International, "War without End: The Price of Inaction in Syria," April 4, 2013

Christoph Reuter

translated from the German by Ella Ornstein

TAKE A MOMENT TO IMAGINE THINGS THIS WAY: A Syrian dictator with a full beard—an Islamist harboring al-Qaida sympathies—has the Christian population of his country shot, starved, and bombed, lets fanatical militias massacre non-believers and burns the country down to ashes. Were that the case, an alliance of Western nations would step up to intervene faster than you could say "Mali."

Yet the people of Syria have been trying to rid themselves of a dictator for two years now. They spent months getting shot at while participating in peaceful demonstrations before they started putting up armed resistance, and now they are facing a regime that intends to annihilate them. But it would seem that they're simply out of luck.

The reason isn't hard to see: Most of these rebels are Sunnis or, more broadly, Muslims. Many of them also have beards and shout "Allahu akbar" (as do the much smaller numbers of Ismailis, Druzes and Christians who fight alongside them). Sunnis also live in the areas that are being bombed almost daily when visibility is good.

Muslims rising up against their rulers to demand justice simply doesn't fit into our worldview. Over the past decades, this view has been fed on news of the Taliban, of radical Islamist clerics preaching messages of hate, of "honor" killings, of battles over a Danish cartoon, and of the events of 9/11. Held responsible for the sum total of all we have heard over the years, Syria's Muslims are finding that the world views their struggle with suspicion and as just another attempt to establish a Muslim theocracy.

If they were Tibetans, you could be sure things would be different. But, as is, Bashar Assad's air force has been allowed to bomb with impunity. Scud missiles level entire city blocks, while Syria gradually empties out. Over 70,000 people have died in the conflict, and more than 1 million have fled the country.

From the start, Assad's regime has played on the West's fears expertly. It has denounced Syrian protestors as foreign jihadists—while simultaneously releasing hundreds of al-Qaida supporters from prisons. It has faked attacks and worked to incite the country's various religious groups against one another, only to then turn around and present itself as a secular bulwark against radicalism.

And the regime's message finds willing ears in the West, where the fact that Assad bears primary responsibility for all this murder is dutifully mentioned. But, of course, the latter is only done as a prelude to enumerating, incident by incident, human rights abuses on the part of the rebels, in order to arrive at the conclusion that both sides in the conflict are terrible.

Should ... Should ... Should

The West doesn't want to intervene. In Germany, both the government and the opposition have assumed the stance that, in addition to not providing the rebels with military aid, it should also stringently uphold the E.U.'s arms embargo. Yet it's not as if the Syrian opposition has always been clamoring for weapons at all costs. Instead, asking for them is more of a last resort now that all its other appeals to the international community—for everything from a military intervention to a no-fly zone—have been turned down.

Despite a number of successes on the rebels' part, the regime's troops still hold the city centers of almost all major cities. They have also held on to enough airports to allow them to carry out strikes on the regions of the country that have been liberated, something they do continually. Assad no longer has anything to gain in this conflict, but there is still plenty he can destroy.

Very slowly, the West is coming around to a different perspective. The United States has been covertly providing aid since late fall, flying arms and ammunition into Turkey—3,500 tons' worth, according to the *New York Times*—to be delivered from there to Syrian rebel groups. However, not many of those supplies seemed to have arrived by late January, when rebel commanders in northern Syria were still issuing their fighters individual, carefully counted rounds of ammunition. The rebels urgently need anti-aircraft missiles to defend themselves against air strikes, but Washington is holding back on supplying such weapons, afraid they might eventually fall into the wrong hands. Great Britain and France now want to supply the rebels with arms, but the EU embargo is still in place—and Germany still supporting it.

How, then, can the inferno in this land that was once Syria be brought to an end? Supporters

of the embargo come up with all sorts of declara-
tions, all of which seem to employ the same verb:
"Assad should resign!" "We should support the UN's
mission in Syria!" "We should prevent Russia from
further arming Assad!" "We should make clear to
those who support the Islamists that they had better stop doing so."

We should, but apparently we can't—and therein
lies the problem. To base our policies on airy appeals
that haven't produced any results in the last two years
is merely self-deception.

Illogical Arguments

There are many good reasons to refrain from
military involvement in other countries. In the case
of Syria, however, some of the rationales put forth
are simply illogical. For example, there is the argument that there are already so many weapons in the
country that it doesn't make sense to send in any
more. By that logic, we could have spared ourselves
the invasion of Afghanistan, not to mention the en-

tire arms race conducted in recent decades.

The curious thing about many German politicians is that they continue to praise Germany's involvement in Afghanistan, even though it has been a failure when measured by its own goals, yet they don't want to intervene militarily in a situation in which it would make sense to do so. In taking this stance, these politicians are ignoring one fundamental difference: In Afghanistan in 2001 and in Iraq in 2003, there was no revolution from within, no vision of a different form of government; instead, there was an invasion from outside. The U.S. was able to topple Saddam Hussein and the Taliban, but not to create stable governments to replace them.

Syria is different. The uprising that began here in many different places simultaneously and without centralized leadership gave rise to hundreds of rebel groups that are not subordinate to any single, centralized command, yet manage to cooperate passably well. Committees for self-government have formed in the places where Assad's troops have been driven out. What is in place at the moment is chaotic and inadequate, but people here don't want anarchy. They want a government—just a different one from what they had. Lawyers, businesspeople, religious leaders and civil servants are all doing their best to maintain public order. The question is how long this system will continue to function.

Empty Excuses

Worn down between the regime's brutality and the jihadists who have been growing stronger for months, embittered by the West's passivity and terribly impoverished, some people have turned to brutality, while others have fled. More and more of the rebels have joined with the radicals, not least because these groups receive abundant supplies from networks of influential clerics in the Gulf States. "Ahrar al-Sham"—one of the two largest fundamentalist groups within the rebels' ranks—"always buys the latest weapons, and plenty of them. They have money," a middleman in northern Syria reported in December.

To hold up these Islamists as a reason not to get involved is to confuse cause and effect. And those who defend the arms embargo—as German Chancellor Angela Merkel does on the grounds that supplying the rebels with arms could further fuel the conflict—are misjudging both the nature of the regime and the dynamics at work in this war.

Assad has systematically tested out whether the international community would object to his use of tanks, of military helicopters, of jets and of missiles. U.S. President Barack Obama has drawn a line only at the use of chemical weapons, which taken the other way around amounts to a declaration that the U.S. will not get involved under any other circumstances. Assad and his generals would sooner accept the country's destruction than yield their grip on power. And as long as the West allows them to continue, they will.

This is the prospect we face: an utterly ravaged country, with 6 million instead of 1 million refugees, and a civil war that will drag Lebanon along into the fray—a war that will not end with Assad's downfall, but will continue indefinitely, fueled by a cycle of revenge and retaliation.

Should that happen, Germany's government will of course condemn it vehemently.

*With or Without Us: Why Syria's Future
Is in Its Own Hands*

TIME, May 13, 2013

Fareed Zakaria

THOSE URGING THE U.S. TO INTERVENE IN
Syria are certain of one thing: If we had intervened
sooner, things would be better in that war-torn
country. Had the Obama Administration gotten
involved earlier, there would be less instability and
fewer killings. We would not be seeing, in John
McCain's words of April 28, "atrocities that are on
a scale that we have not seen in a long, long time."

In fact, we have seen atrocities much worse than
those in Syria very recently, in Iraq under U.S. occupation only a few years ago. From 2003 to 2012, despite there being as many as 180,000 American and

allied troops in Iraq, somewhere between 150,000 and 300,000 Iraqi civilians died and about 1.5 million fled the country. Jihadi groups flourished in Iraq, and al-Qaeda had a huge presence there. The U.S. was about as actively engaged in Iraq as is possible, and yet more terrible things happened there than in Syria. Why?

The point here is not to make comparisons among atrocities. The situation in Syria is much like that in Iraq—and bears little resemblance to that in Libya—so we can learn a lot from our experience there. Joshua Landis, the leading scholar on Syria, points out that it is the last of the three countries of the Levant where minority regimes have been challenged by the majority. In Lebanon, the Christian elite were displaced through a bloody civil war that started in the 1970s and lasted 15 years. In Iraq in 2003, the U.S. military quickly displaced the Sunni elite, handing the country over to the Shi'ites—but the Sunnis have fought back ferociously for almost a decade. Sectarian killings persist in Iraq to this day.

Syria is following a similar pattern. The country has a Sunni majority. The regime is Alawite, a Shi'ite subsect that makes up 12% of the population, but it also draws some support from other minorities—Druze, Armenians and others—who worry about their fate in a majoritarian Syria. These fears might be justified. Consider what has happened to the Christians of Iraq. There were as many as 1.4 million of them before the Iraq war. There are now about 500,000, and many of their churches have been destroyed. Christian life in Iraq, which has survived since the days of the Bible, is in real danger of being extinguished by the current regime in Baghdad.

All the features of Syria's civil war that are supposedly the result of U.S. nonintervention also appeared in Iraq despite America's massive intervention there. In Iraq under U.S. occupation, many Sunni groups banded together with jihadi forces from the outside; some even broke bread with al-Qaeda. Shi'ite militias got support from Iran. Both

sides employed tactics that were brutal beyond belief—putting electric drills through people's heads,
burning others alive and dumping still breathing
victims into mass graves.

These struggles get vicious for a reason: the
stakes are very high. The minority regime fights to
the end because it fears for its life once out of power.
The Sunnis of Iraq fought—even against the mighty
American military—because they knew that life under the Shi'ites would be ugly, as it has proved to be.
The Alawites in Syria will fight even harder because
they are a smaller minority and have further to fall.

Would U.S. intervention—no-fly zones, arms,
aid to the opposition forces—make things better?
It depends on what one means by better. It would
certainly intensify the civil war. It would also make
the regime of Bashar Assad more desperate. Perhaps
Assad has already used chemical weapons; with his
back against the wall, he might use them on a larger
scale. As for external instability, Landis points out
that if U.S. intervention tipped the balance against

the Alawites, they might flee Syria into Lebanon, destabilizing that country for decades. Again, this pattern is not unprecedented. Large numbers on the losing side have fled wars in the Middle East, from Palestinians in 1948 to Iraq's Sunnis in the past decade.

If the objective is actually to reduce the atrocities and minimize potential instability, the key will be a political settlement that gives each side an assurance that it has a place in the new Syria. That was never achieved in Iraq, which is why, despite U.S. troops and arms and influence, the situation turned into a violent free-for-all. If some kind of political pact can be reached, there's hope for Syria. If it cannot, U.S. assistance to the rebels or even direct military intervention won't change much: Syria will follow the pattern of Lebanon and Iraq—a long, bloody civil war. And America will be in the middle of it.

The Dangerous Price of Ignoring Syria

New York Times, April 15, 2013

Vali Nasr

PRESIDENT OBAMA HAS DOGGEDLY RESISTED American involvement in Syria. The killing of over 70,000 people and the plight of over a million refugees have elicited sympathy from the White House but not much more. That is because Syria challenges a central aim of Obama's foreign policy: shrinking the U.S. footprint in the Middle East and downplaying the region's importance to global politics. Doing more on Syria would reverse the U.S. retreat from the region.

Since the beginning of Obama's first term, the administration's stance as events unfolded in the

Middle East has been wholly reactive. This "lean back and wait" approach has squandered precious opportunity to influence the course of events in the Middle East. There has been no strategy for capitalizing on the opportunity that the Arab Spring presented, or for containing its fallout—the Syrian crisis being the worst case to date. The president rewarded Burmese generals with a six-hour visit for their willingness to embrace reform, but he has not visited a single Arab country that went through the Arab Spring.

Obama sees Syria as a tragic humanitarian crisis without obvious strategic implications for the United States. "How do I weigh tens of thousands who've been killed in Syria versus the tens of thousands who are currently being killed in the Congo?" he asked in a New Republic interview in January. When the president visited the region last month he chose to focus on the Arab-Israeli peace process rather than Syria. The peace process is now at the top of Secretary of State John Kerry's agenda.

The plight of Palestinians is a perennial concern, but it is in Syria that the future of the region hangs in the balance. Choosing the peace process over Syria underscores not the administration's interest in the Middle East but its determination to look past it.

Washington has wasted precious time in using diplomatic, economic and military levers to influence the course of events in Syria. That neglect has allowed the conflagration to rage at great human cost, radicalizing the opposition and putting at risk U.S. allies across the region.

America cannot and should not decide the fate of the Middle East, but it should be clear about its stakes there, and not shy away from efforts to at least nudge events in more favorable directions as this critical region faces momentous choices. A "lean back and wait" posture toward unfolding events is dangerous.

The paroxysm of violence in Syria is expected to kill tens of thousands more and produce as many as three million refugees by the year's end. That is a humanitarian tragedy to be sure, but one with immediate strategic consequences. American insouciance in the face of that devastation is fomenting anti-Americanism. The waves of refugees will constitute an unstable population that will be a breeding ground for extremism and in turn destabilize the countries where they take refuge. Syria's neighbors are not equipped to deal with a humanitarian disaster on this scale.

The longer the devastation goes on the more difficult it will be to put Syria back together, and failing to do so will leave a dangerous morass in the heart of the Middle East, a failed state at war with itself where extremism and instability will fester and all manner of terrorists and Al Qaeda affiliates will find ample space, resources and recruits to menace the region and world.

Worse yet, the conflict in Syria could spill over its borders. Syria has become ground zero in a broader conflict that pits Shiites against Sunnis and shapes the larger regional competition for power between

Iran, Turkey, and Saudi Arabia. Syria's paroxysms if allowed to drag on could potentially spread far and wide and even change the map of the region. America may think it does not have any interests in Syria, but it has interests everywhere the Syrian conflict touches.

Lebanon and Iraq are each deeply divided along sectarian lines, and both countries teeter on a knife's edge as tensions rise between their ascendant Shiite populations who fear a setback if Bashar al-Assad falls, and the minority Sunnis in their own countries who support Syria's Sunni-led opposition. Sectarian tensions stretch from Lebanon and Iraq through the Gulf countries of Saudi Arabia, Kuwait, and Bahrain and on to Pakistan where sectarian violence has exploded into the open.

It is time America takes the lead in organizing international assistance to refugees. America should not hide behind the Russian veto. It should pursue a concerted diplomatic strategy in support of arming the rebels and imposing a no-flight zone over

Syria. That would not only hamper Assad's ability to fight, it would allow refugees to remain within Syria's borders, thus reducing pressure on neighboring countries.

It is time the U.S. took over from Qatar and Saudi Arabia in organizing the Syrian opposition into a credible political force—failure to do that accounts for the chaos that has paralyzed the group. There are powerful economic sanctions that the U.S. could use to cripple the Assad regime.

Finally, America should build ties with the Free Syrian Army with the goal of denying extremist groups the ability to dominate the armed resistance and gaining influence with groups that will dominate Syria's future. It was failing to build those ties in Afghanistan that allowed the resistance groups who opposed the Soviet Union to disintegrate into the Taliban and Al Qaeda.

The Syrian crisis has become a Gordian knot that cannot be easily disentangled. As daunting as the crisis looks, there is a cost to inaction—in human suffering, regional instability and damage to America's global standing. And as the Syrian crisis escalates, America and the world will only rediscover their stakes in the Middle East. If Obama truly wants to pivot away from the Middle East then he has to help end the bloodletting in Syria.

Syria, Savagery, and Self-Determination:
What the Anti-Interventionists Are Missing

Nader Hashemi

THERE IS A WIDE BODY OF OPINION AGAINST arming the Syrian rebels. These voices, especially those on the Left, argue that pursuing a military defeat of the Assad regime is mistaken and misguided because it increases civilian suffering and prolongs the conflict. Stephen Zunes, for example, has argued that "it is critical to not allow the understandably strong emotional reaction to the ongoing carnage lead to policies that could end up making things worse." In response to the question of what should be done about the nightmare in Syria, he has written that the "short answer, unfortunately, is not much."[41] Alternatively, it is suggested that negotiating with Damascus and engaging Russia and Iran in diplomacy offer the only way out of the Syrian predicament.[42]

While these arguments are attractive and appeal to our best Gandhian impulses, upon closer examination they represent a fundamental misreading of Syria. If pursued they will not end the conflict but will likely prolong it, mainly because these prescriptions ignore two key elements at the core of this dispute: 1) the nature of the Assad regime and 2) the right to self-determination of the Syrian people.

The Assad Regime's Criminal Enterprise

The revolution in Syria was born out of the 2011 Arab Spring. It began nonviolently and for the same reasons as the other uprisings in North Africa and the Middle East. The core aspirations of the protesters were the same: *hurriya* (political freedom), *adala ijtima'iyya* (social justice) and *karama* (dignity). What was different, however, was the nature of the regime they faced.

A comparison of the human rights records of member states of the Arab League places Syria at the extreme end of a spectrum of repression. Arguably, only Saddam Hussein's Iraq was worse. While the 1982 massacre in Hama is frequently cited to highlight the viciousness of the Assad regime, less well known are the horrors of Syria's prison system. Tens of thousands have passed through its doors. Untold numbers never made it out. A 1996 Human Rights Watch report on the notorious Tadmor prison describes "deaths under torture" and "summary executions on a massive scale." One former inmate described the place as a "kingdom of death and madness" whose emaciated prisoners were compared to "survivors of Nazi concentration camps."[43]

But this was just one jail in a veritable archipelago. The full story of Syria's prison system and internal human rights nightmare under the Assads has yet to be properly told. When the full truth emerges it will evoke the horrors Alexandr Solzhenitsyn chronicled in *The Gulag Archipelago*. Pieces of the truth, however, are slowly emerging. A recent Human Rights Watch report, revealingly titled *Torture Archipelago*, provided new details on the scale, breadth and depth of Syria's human rights nightmare. These abuses are so enormous that they constitute, according to Human Rights Watch, "crimes against humanity" and have earned Assad a referral to the International Criminal Court.[44] Given this background, Damascus' ruthless response to peaceful demands for change in March 2011 were entirely predictable.

In the first few months of the uprising—well before the creation of the Free Syrian Army and before there was an Al Qaeda presence on the ground—more than two thousand Syrian civilians were killed. Over ten thousand more were arrested during the same period and taken to notoriously ghastly detention centers.[45] By the first anniversary of the revolution Assad had crossed the proverbial Rubicon. All the leading human rights organizations—Amnesty International, Human Rights Watch, and the UN Human Rights Council's Independent International Commission of Inquiry on the Syrian Arab Republic—unanimously and unambiguously charged the Syrian government with a state-sanctioned policy of "war crimes" and "crimes against humanity."[46] As the carnage continued, according to the UN, more than 60,000 people had been killed by early 2013.[47] The Assad regime is now in the same moral category as the Bosnian Serb war criminal Radovan Karadzic and Rwanda's Hutu generals.

Syria is unlike other countries that have experienced civilian revolts during the Arab Spring. The level of regime-orchestrated violence—replete with cluster bombs, Scud missiles, sexual violence, indiscriminate attacks on bread lines, hospitals, universities, homes, and children, and now apparently chemical weapons—is on an order and magnitude that is incomparable with other regional countries that have been shaken by the Arab Spring.[48] Thus what arguably worked in Yemen's "managed transition" does not apply to Syria. The cases are qualitatively different from a human rights perspective. If the history of ending massive state-sanctioned atrocities is any guide—Tanzania's intervention in Uganda, India's in East Pakistan, Vietnam's in Cambodia, the Rwandan Patriotic Front's in Rwanda, NATO's in Bosnia and Kosovo—massive bloodshed constituting war crimes and crimes against humanity are not brought to an end by negotiating with the perpetrating regime, nor by engaging in diplomacy with allied countries that are complicit in these events. Military force is required.

Dignity and Self-Determination

The theme of dignity, or its converse, indignity, and it relationship to modern Arab politics is a multi-dimensional phenomenon. It exists at both the individual and the collective levels. Syrians immediately identified with the self-immolation of Mohammed Bouazizi in Tunisia, whose martyrdom ignited the Arab Spring.[49] His economic plight was theirs. His frustration, humiliation, and anger under the crushing weight of dictatorship resonated and struck a deep personal chord. But the theme of "Arab indignity" also exists on a collective level, and it is associated with a set of common historical experiences, which partly explains why it is such a potent force in the politics of the region.

For the Arab-Islamic world, in which Syria figures centrally, the 20th century was an extremely bitter one. European colonialism and imperialism thwarted the aspirations for self-determination of millions of Arabs. The desire to create one pan-Arab state from the ruins of the Ottoman Empire's Arabic-speaking provinces was dashed at the altar of British and French ambition. The state system that emerged after World War I reflected the economic and geostrategic interests of London and Paris more than it did popular preference on the streets of Cairo or Damascus. The birth of the modern Arab world thus engendered bitter memories and poisoned relations between Muslim societies and Western ones. This was compounded by Western support for the national rights of Jewish settlers in Palestine over those of the indigenous Palestinian population—the legacy of which continues to afflict the region and indeed the world to this day.

The aftermath of World War II saw the gradual loosening of European control of the Arab world and the emergence of a brief moment of optimism. Many thought that an opportunity had finally arrived for the realization of meaningful self-determination. But this opening did not last long. The region soon found itself awash in military coups and single-party states. Syria got the Ba'ath Party. Within the span of a couple of decades, a new postcolonial elite came to power and a familiar political landscape took shape. Yes, the new rulers were native to the soil and had Muslim-sounding names, but they behaved in ways that were eerily familiar. A new chasm between state and society developed that replicated the old colonial one, only this time the ruling elites were Arabs rather than Europeans.

The term neocolonialism is an apt description for this state of affairs. The Syrian writer Rana Kabbani has used the phrase "internal colonialism" to describe the authoritarian rule of postcolonial elites in the Arab world. She explains that 42 years of one-family rule in Syria is "much like the external colonialism of the past, [it] has robbed them and bombed them and impeded them from joining the free peoples of the world."[50] The Syrian human rights activist and opposition leader Radwan Ziadeh has similarly argued that we "need a second independence in Syria. The first was from the French and the second will be from the Assad dynasty."[51]

Commenting on this core feature of Arab political life, the historian Ilan Pappé has referred to the Arab Spring as the "second phase of decolonization." What recent events have demonstrated, he notes, is the collective "assertion of self-dignity in the Arab world" after decades of humiliation, despotism, and despair.[52]

This is what the Syrian revolution is fundamentally about and why Assad and his mafia state must go. The Syrian intellectual Burhan Ghalioun picks up on this point that negotiations with Damascus are futile. The "existence of the [Assad] regime is like an invasion of the state, a colonisation of society" where "hundreds of intellectuals are forbidden to travel, 150,000 have gone into exile and 17,000 have either disappeared or been imprisoned for expressing their opinion . . . It is impossible (for President Bashar al-Assad) to say (like Mubarak and Ben Ali) 'I will not prolong or renew my mandate' like other presidents have pretended to do—because Syria is, for Assad, his private family property, the word 'country' is not part of the vocabulary."[53]

It is precisely this point that the anti-interventionists are missing. This is a fascist regime embodied in the oft heard slogans: "God, Bashar, Syria, and Nothing Else" and "Assad or we burn down the country!" It is not amenable to compromise or negotiation. For them it is a zero-sum game and a fight to the finish. It cynically manipulates sectarian identity and anti-imperialism to maintain its criminal enterprise. Military intervention, as regrettable and complicated as it may be, is the only way to stop Assad's killing machine. By doing so it may also open the door for the people of Syria to exercise, arguably for the first time in their modern history, their right to self-determination.

But there is a further compelling reason why military intervention in Syria is required: this is what most Syrians are demanding from the international community. The most inclusive and representative body of Syrians is the National Coalition for Syrian Revolutionary and Opposition Forces (the Syrian Coalition, for short). While far from a perfect group, it harbors the best prospects for leading Syria to a democratic future. It includes Syrians both inside and outside the country and spans the religious-secular divide. More than 110 countries have officially recognized it as "the legitimate representative of the Syrian people."[54]

The Syrian Coalition has been pleading for a Libya-style intervention (no boots on the ground, a no-fly/no-kill zone, arming the moderate elements of the Syrian rebels). On April 24, 2013 they issued the following clarion call to the world:

> The Syrian Coalition finds it tragic that NATO has the power to stop further loss of life in Syria, but chooses not to take that course of action....The international community must rise to its great moral and ethical responsibilities and put an end to this bloodshed. History will not only condemn the murderous criminals, but also those who had the power to intervene but chose to be idle.[55]

Today, Syria is a litmus test for the Left, which has long championed the rights of oppressed peoples in the developing world. If we truly believe in the right to self-determination for these people— the Syrian people included—then we are morally obligated to listen to them. We must follow *their* lead when it comes to deeply divisive issues such as military intervention. In the end, their needs—at this critical moment in their history—are far more important than our preferences and need for ideological purity.

Conclusion

Putting Syria back together again will take a long time. There are no quick fixes or easy answers. The trauma and devastation wrought by the Assad years will take generations to overcome. Populations that have lived under a police state for decades rarely emerge from the experience with liberal sensibilities. New political habits and social mores will have to be cultivated.

And the legacy of the current war and its wounds will take a long time to heal. A formidable challenge that lies ahead is accommodating the legitimate fears of minority communities, especially the Alawites and Christians, and assuring them that they will have a secure future in a post-Assad Syria. This challenge is compounded by the rise of radical

Salafist and jihadi groups, who will have to be confronted and disarmed. The policies of regional powers—Saudi Arabia, Iran, and Israel—pose a further challenge. For different reasons, none of them wants to see a prosperous and democratic Syria emerge.

But the first step required in getting Syria on the path toward stability and self-determination is the removal of the Assad regime. This is what the Arab Spring is about; this is what most Syrians want. It is a precondition for a lasting peace; without it the war will continue and both Syria and the rest of the Middle East will plunge even deeper into this nightmare of bloodshed and chaos.

From Dayton to Damascus

New York Times, "When to Talk to Monsters,"
May 13, 2013

Christopher R. Hill

CRITICS OF U.S. PRESIDENT BARACK OBAMA'S handling of the Syrian crisis increasingly argue that the problem is his administration's reluctance to intervene militarily. In fact, the problem lies elsewhere—in the administration's unwillingness to lead a sustained and substantial diplomatic effort to identify political arrangements that could offer Syrians a way out of civil war. That process, not American bombs, brought about the end of the war in Bosnia in the 1990s—an experience that remains relevant today.

The narrative of the two-year Syrian crisis has been dominated by the question of whether America should become involved militarily, as if armed intervention would bring a quick and decisive conclusion to this most brutal of civil wars. Arming the opposition, declaring and patrolling a no-fire zone, aerial bombardment, and "boots on the ground" have all been suggested as potential means to end the conflict.

As the carnage mounts, anger at the Obama administration's supposed inaction intensifies, as does disagreement within the Obama cabinet about what to do. Earlier this spring, we learned—bizarrely, from off-hand testimony by former Defense Secretary Leon Panetta—that he supported a "CIA plan" to arm the opposition. Secretary of State Hillary Clinton chimed in that she, too, supported the CIA, though precisely what it was that she and Panetta supported remains shrouded in mystery. The statements created the unsettling impression that Obama was at odds with his national-security officials.

Now the two-year narrative of indecision has been merged with that of a reluctant warrior—a president who is uncomfortable with the use of American power, even after his own "red line" in Syria was crossed. Obama had said that the use of chemical weapons in Syria would be a "game changer" demanding a U.S. military response; but, despite evidence of their use, Obama has refused to follow through on his threat. To his critics, Obama seems to be weakening America's reputation by demonstrating a lack of resolve.

But those who are so interested in military intervention in Syria today would do well to consider who will rule Syria tomorrow, because that uncertainty is what fuels the conflict. Syrians on both sides of the civil war are certainly thinking about it. They desperately need greater clarity about how their country will be governed in the future.

Will it be a federal state with regional autonomy and enclaves for Christians, Kurds, and Druze? Will it be a unitary state, controlled (again) by a heavy hand in Damascus, perhaps this time a sectarian Sunni government?

Early on, the US irrevocably broke ties with Syrian President Bashar al-Assad's government, branding Assad the culprit in the conflict and declaring that he must go. Nothing about Assad's behavior since then would merit reconsideration of that decision; nonetheless, one can ask whether the U.S. has thus relegated itself to the thankless and secondary task of refereeing among opposition groups whose capacity for disagreement seemingly knows no limit.

While Syria is indeed divided between a dictatorship and a democratic opposition, that is only one fault line; there are many more. The patchwork quilt of ethnicity and sectarian identity suggests that ruling Syria would not be an easy task for anyone.

A future democratic leader in Syria will face extraordinary problems. With the Assad regime's legacy so fresh in people's minds, will Syrians want a weak central government? What will the parliament look like? Will representation be purely proportional, or will some kind of upper house be needed to ensure that minorities (Druze, Kurds, etc.) do not feel overwhelmed by the Sunni majority?

Likewise, one can easily imagine, given the country's history, that there will be demands to disband the military (civilian control is all well and good, except that the Assads were civilians). Would that be a good idea?

At the risk of stating the obvious, it might be worth getting some of this on paper in the form of an international plan.

It is customary—and sometimes accurate—to suggest that brutal regimes are alien to a country, the result of an unhappy confluence of circumstances in which the bad guys somehow emerged the victors. Thus, sooner or later, depending on when and how much U.S. military power is applied, those unfortunate circumstances can be reversed, and the country returned to "normal." In fact, it is often the failure to create workable political arrangements that leads to dictatorship in the first place.

This is where Bosnia is instructive. The war

there did not end as a result of the application of punitive U.S. military force. Nor did it end because leaders gathered around a table in Dayton, Ohio. The outcome may have been a cliff-hanger at the end; but, given the months of exhaustive work that preceded the actual peace conference, the gathering was merely an elaborate signing ceremony.

Indeed, the participants in Dayton rarely even met face to face. Most of the political arrangements, and even most of the map, were hammered out before the Dayton conference through shuttle diplomacy and bilateral meetings in support of a plan backed by the so-called Contact Group, consisting of the U.S., the United Kingdom, France, Russia, and Germany.

A similar international peace process—bringing people around an idea rather than a table—is what the situation in Syria demands. When Syrians know what the outcome will be, they will stop fighting and reach a settlement, because no one wants to be the last to die in a civil war.

Better Assad Than the Islamists?
Why the "Argument from Islamism" Is Wrong

Thomas Pierret

ONE OF THE MOST COMMON ARGUMENTS against Western involvement in the Syrian conflict is that Islamists dominate the armed opposition. From this point of view, the Assad regime is seen as a secular bulwark that should be preserved until a political agreement is reached or, more cynically, until the two sides achieve mutual destruction. This approach relies on the assumption that no credible alternative to the radical Islamists exists among the rebels and that any kind of intervention would therefore empower forces that are inimical to both democratic values and Western interests.

As for the beleaguered but resilient Assad we know today, he is certainly no bulwark against Islamists; in fact his brutal and sectarian war on the opposition has played into the hands of the most militant Salafi factions, which have thrived across the country over the last year. In other words, "better Assad than the Islamists" actually means "both Assad and the (radical) Islamists."

Opposing foreign intervention because of the strength of Islamists is wrong for at least two other reasons. First, because the lack of foreign intervention in support for the Syrian opposition is precisely what has favored the spectacular rise of radical Islamists during the second year of the uprising. Secondly, evidence exists that it is actually possible to bolster more moderate alternatives by providing them carefully managed logistical support. As I will explain below in more detail, non-Salafi groups have been the main beneficiaries of the significant influx of Croatian weapons that was engineered in late 2012 by the Arab and Western allies of the opposition.

But there was nothing inevitable in the rise of the al-Qaeda-related al-Nusra front and other Salafi groups like Ahrar al-Sham. The first armed groups that were established by military defectors in the summer of 2011 were not "secular" in the strict sense, as several of them were given religious names, but their discourse was moderate and did not include any distinctly Islamist agenda. They were widely popular though, as no strong demand for a more radical orientation existed at that time.

The first half of 2012 marked a watershed in the process of Islamization of the revolution. This radicalization was a direct by-product of the Assad regime's decision to use its full military might against rebellious cities (heavy artillery was first used in Homs in February 2012, and the first airstrikes were carried out on Aleppo in July). Furthermore, sectarian massacres targeting Sunni civilians enhanced the process of radicalization. Sectarian polarization and a widespread sense of abandonment by an impotent West combined to create a fertile ground for radical Islamist ideas. Foreign fighters began to flow into Syria for the same reasons: although seasoned itinerant jihadis would certainly have joined the struggle whatever happened, the escalation of the conflict and the corollary atrocities against civilians convinced large numbers of hitherto not-so-radical foreign volunteers to take up arms in support of their Syrian brethren.

The second factor behind the rise of radical Islamists is the issue of funding. Common wisdom has it that the Islamization of the insurgency has been favored by the support of conservative Gulf monarchies, namely Saudi Arabia and Qatar. The reality is very different, however. Despite Qatar's partnership with the Muslim Brotherhood, the latter's military arm in Syria, the Committee of the Shields of the Revolution, apparently suffers from a dire need of financial means. Apart from that, the Brothers have "shares" in powerful insurgent groups such as the Tawhid Brigade in Aleppo and the Faruq Battalions, but they do not own them. As for Saudi

Arabia, it has constantly backed the establishment of coordination structures run by relatively secular defector officers such as Mustafa al-Sheikh's Military Council, Hussein al-Hajj Ali's Syrian National Army, Mahir al-Nu'aymi's Joint Command of the Military Councils, and Salim Idris' Joint Command of the Free Syrian Army. In the province of Idlib, Riyadh's chief client is none of the three local Salafi heavyweights (Ahrar al-Sham, Suqur al-Sham and Jabhat al-Nusra), but their more secular rivals of Shuhada' Suriyya.

In fact, Islamization has not resulted from funding by Gulf states, but from the lack of it. Although arms paid for by Saudi Arabia and Qatar started to make their way into Syria in the spring of 2012, insufficient quantities, sudden disruptions of deliveries and poor management of their distribution plagued the opposition's military effort throughout the rest of the year.[56] In such circumstances, Gulf-based private networks of funding have played a prominent role in the bankrolling of the insurgency, and groups with privileged access to these networks have frequently outgunned less connected ones. Gulf benefactors, being generally of a Salafi persuasion, have logically favored like-minded outfits and encouraged others to "Salafize" their outlook.[57]

Only in late 2012 did Gulf states significantly step up their support for the Syrian rebels, an effort that quickly translated into the empowerment of non-Salafi battalions. Croatian antitank weapons purchased with Saudi money were channeled to selected insurgent groups, primarily in the southern province of Deraa (through Jordanian intelligence), but also, from Turkey, in the center and north of the country. Results were especially spectacular in Deraa, as rebels achieved significant gains in a region which until then had remained under the firm grip of loyalist forces.[58]

Remarkably, insurgent successes in the south were predominantly achieved by groups that claim to be part of the Free Syrian Army and raise Syrian flags (Shuhada al-Yarmuk Brigade, Fajr al-Islam

Brigade, al-Omari Brigade), two features that clearly distinguish them from Salafi organisations. A similar pattern was replicated in other parts of the country in April, as FSA-related groups seized the airport of al-Dab'a (Homs) and captured parts of the bases of Abu al-Dhuhur (Idlib) and Kweyris (Aleppo). This upsurge in the military activities of non-Salafi insurgents was all the more remarkable in that in previous months, Jabhat al-Nusra and Ahrar al-Sham had been chiefly responsible for most major insurgent victories in the North (airports of Taftanaz and al-Jirah, city of al-Raqqa).

Such developments show that fears of military help falling in the "wrong hands" are not necessarily more justified than the claim that the Afghan precedent will necessarily repeat itself in Syria. It was not US support that favored the rise of the most radical elements among the Afghan Mujahidin in the 1980s, but the fact that this support was mediated by Pakistani intelligence, a quite unreliable partner in that respect. Things can turn out to be different provided one chooses intermediaries that are determined to contain radical Islamism, as is obviously the case with Jordanian intelligence.

Western-Arab support for FSA-related battalions has sometimes been derided as a replication of the Awakening Councils established by the U.S. in Iraq.[59] The comparison is misguided, however. Syrian groups were not "created" as a counterweight to Salafi organizations; rather, they were the early mainstream of the insurgency, only waiting for someone to help them. Of course, these battalions are not necessarily "secular" by Western standards, but their stance on issues such as democracy and foreign policy are undeniably more flexible than those of their Salafi counterparts.

To be sure, supporting them is no guarantee that Islamists will not prevail in a post-Assad Syria. However, this should not prevent the West from hastening Assad's fall by all necessary means. First, because it is a fantasy to think that any political arrangement in an Arab country could achieve stability by excluding moderate Islamists. Second, because the real choice is not between Assad's doomed "panzer-secularism" (secularism imposed by tanks) and Islamism; it is rather between a pluralistic (even if predominantly religious-conservative) Syrian society that can still be preserved by acting quickly, and extreme versions of Salafi Islam that will continue to flourish if Syria remains abandoned by the outside world to its current apocalyptic fate.

THOMAS PIERRET   253

ABOUT THE CONTRIBUTORS

Asli Bâli is Associate Professor of Law at UCLA School of Law. She worked for the United Nations in Gaza and for the World Bank in the West Bank.

Richard Falk is Professor Emeritus of International Law at Princeton University and Visiting Distinguished Professor in Global and International Studies at the University of California, Santa Barbara. The United Nations Special Rapporteur on Palestinian human rights, his books include *The International Law of Civil War, Human Rights and State Sovereignty*, and *The Costs of War: International Law, the UN, and World Order after Iraq.*

Tom Farer is University Professor and former Dean of the University of Denver's Josef Korbel School of International Studies. The former president of the Inter-American Commission on Human Rights of the OAS, the University of New Mexico, and the Association of Professional Schools of International Affairs, his most recent book is *Confronting Global Terrorism and American Neo-Conservatism: The Framework of a Liberal Grand Strategy.*

CHARLES GLASS was chief Middle East correspondent for ABC News from 1983 to 1993. He is the author of *Tribes with Flags: Adventure and Kidnap in Greater Syria, The Tribes Triumphant: Return Journey to the Middle East, The Northern Front: A Wartime Diary, Money for Old Rope: Disorderly Compositions, Americans in Paris: Life and Death under Nazi Occupation 1940–1944,* and *The Deserters: A Hidden History of World War II.*

SHADI HAMID is Director of Research at the Brookings Doha Center and a fellow at the Saban Center for Middle East Policy at the Brookings Institution.

NADER HASHEMI is Director of the Center for Middle East Studies and Associate Professor of Middle East and Islamic Politics at the University of Denver's Josef Korbel School of International Studies. He is the author of *Islam, Secularism, and Liberal Democracy: Toward a Democratic Theory for Muslim Societies* and co-editor of *The People Reloaded: The Green Movement and the Struggle for Iran's Future*.

CHRISTOPHER R. HILL was U.S. Assistant Secretary of State for East Asia; US Ambassador to Iraq, South Korea, Macedonia, and Poland; US special envoy for Kosovo; a negotiator of the Dayton Peace Accords; and chief US negotiator with North Korea. He is currently Dean of the University of Denver's Josef Korbel School of International Studies and writes a column for *Project Syndicate*.

MICHAEL IGNATIEFF teaches international politics at Harvard University's Kennedy School of Government and the University of Toronto's Munk School of Global

Affairs. He was Leader of the Liberal Party of Canada from 2008 to 2011 and served in the Parliament of Canada from 2006 to 2011. He helped author *The Responsibility to Protect*, the report of the International Commission on Intervention and State Sovereignty.

Afra Jalabi is a Montreal-based Syrian writer. She serves on the Executive Committee of The Day After project, an international working group of Syrians representing a large spectrum of the country's opposition engaged in an independent transition planning process, and she was a signatory to the Damascus Declaration, an umbrella group that aimed to improve human rights and create gradual change in Syria.

Rafif Jouejati is the English spokeswoman for the Local Coordination Committees of Syria, a network of activists throughout the country. She is the director of FREE-Syria, a nonprofit humanitarian organization that focuses on women's empowerment, and a member of The Day After Project, an international working group of Syrians representing a large spectrum of the country's opposition engaged in an independent transition planning process.

MARY KALDOR is Professor of Global Governance and Director of the Civil Society and Human Security Research Unit at the London School of Economics. A columnist for openDemocracy.net, her books include *The Ultimate Weapon is No Weapon: Human Security and the Changing Rules of War and Peace, New and Old Wars: Organized Violence in a Global Era,* and *Global Civil Society: An Answer to War.*

MARC LYNCH is Professor of Political Science and International Affairs at George Washington University's Elliott School of International Affairs, where he is the director of the Institute for Middle East Studies and the Project on Middle East Political Science (POMEPS). He is the author of *The Arab Uprising: The Unfinished Revolutions of the New Middle East* and edits the Middle East Channel on ForeignPolicy.com.

VALI NASR is Dean and Professor of International Relations at the Johns Hopkins University's Paul H. Nitze School of Advanced International Studies, and served as special adviser to Ambassador Richard Holbrooke, President Obama's Special Representative for Afghanistan and Pakistan. His books include *The Dispensable Nation: American Foreign Policy in Retreat* and *The Shia Revival: How Conflicts within Islam Will Shape the Future*.

THOMAS PIERRET is Lecturer in Contemporary Islam in the Department of Islamic and Middle Eastern Studies at the University of Edinburgh. He is the author of *Religion and State in Syria: The Sunni Ulama from Coup to Revolution* and co-editor of *Ethnographies of Islam: Ritual Performances and Everyday Practices*.

DANNY POSTEL is Associate Director of the Center for Middle East Studies at the University of Denver. His books include *Reading "Legitimation Crisis" in Tehran: Iran and the Future of Liberalism* and *The*

People Reloaded: The Green Movement and the Struggle for Iran's Future. He is a contributing editor of *Logos: A Journal of Modern Society & Culture* and blogs for *Critical Inquiry*, *Truthout*, and the *Huffington Post*.

Aziz Rana is Associate Professor of Law at Cornell Law School. He is the author of *The Two Faces of American Freedom* and *No Other Gods: The Rise of Constitutional Nationalism in America* (forthcoming).

Christoph Reuter, foreign correspondent for the German magazine *Der Spiegel*, has made ten journeys across Syria since the start of the revolution. He was the first Western journalist to go to Houla to investigate the massacre there. He is the author of *My Life Is a Weapon: A Modern History of Suicide Bombing*.

Kenneth Roth is the executive director of Human Rights Watch. He has conducted numerous human rights investigations and missions around the world and has written extensively on a wide range of human rights abuses, devoting special attention to international justice, counterterrorism, the foreign policies of the major powers, and the work of the United Nations.

ANNE-MARIE SLAUGHTER is president of the New America Foundation and a contributing editor of *The Atlantic*. A professor emerita of Politics and International Affairs at Princeton University and former Dean of the university's Woodrow Wilson School of Public and International Affairs, she served as Director of Policy Planning for the United States Department of State 2009–2011.

FAREED ZAKARIA is the host of CNN's *Fareed Zakaria GPS*, Editor at Large of *TIME*, and a columnist for the *Washington Post*. Formerly the editor of *Newsweek International* and managing editor of *Foreign Affairs*, his books include *The Post-American World* and *The Future of Freedom: Illiberal Democracy at Home and Abroad*, which has been translated into 20 languages.

Radwan Ziadeh is the Executive Director of the Syrian Center for Political and Strategic Studies in Washington, Director of the Damascus Center for Human Rights Studies in Syria, and Managing Editor of the Transitional Justice in the Arab World Project. His most recent book is *Power and Policy in Syria: Intelligence Services, Foreign Relations and Democracy in the Modern Middle East.*

Stephen Zunes is Professor of Politics and International Studies at the University of San Francisco, and chairs the university's program in Middle Eastern Studies. He is a senior policy analyst for the Foreign Policy in Focus project of the Institute for Policy Studies. His books include *Tinderbox: U.S. Foreign Policy and the Roots of Terrorism, Western Sahara: War, Nationalism, and Conflict Irresolution,* and *Nonviolent Social Movements.*

Notes

Nader Hashemi and Danny Postel

[1] "Updated Statistical Analysis of Documentation of Killings in the Syrian Arab Republic," report commissioned by the Office of the UN High Commissioner for Human Rights, June 13, 2013, http://www.ohchr.org/Documents/Countries/SY/HRDAG-Updated-SY-report.pdf. Also see Ian Black, "Syrian deaths near 100,000, says UN—and 6,000 are children," *The Guardian*, June 13, 2013, and "Syria death toll tops 100,000," *The Telegraph*, June 26, 2013 www.telegraph.co.uk/news/worldnews/middleeast/syria/10142892/Syria-death-toll-tops-100000.html.

[2] Michelle Nichols, "Syrians fleeing war at rate not seen since Rwandan genocide: U.N." Reuters, July 16, 2013 www.reuters.com/article/2013/07/16/us-syria-crisis-un-idUS-BRE96F11120130716.

[3] Michelle Nichols, "Syria death toll likely near 70,000, says UN rights chief," Reuters, February 12, 2013.

[4] "Pillay renews call to refer Syria to world criminal court," Office of the United Nations High Commissioner for Human Rights, February 13, 2013, www.ohchr.org/EN/NewsEvents/Pages/Pillay-ToSecurityCouncil.aspx. From March 2011 to May 2013 Amnesty International has published sixteen reports on Syria, Human Rights Watch seven, and the UN Independent International Commission of Inquiry on Syria four, all available on their respective websites.

[5] Desmond Tutu, "We are shamed by Syria's suffering," March 25, 2013, http://theelders.org/article/we-are-all-shamed-syrias-suffering.

[6] Samantha Power, *"A Problem from Hell": America and the Age of Genocide* (New York: Basic Books, 2002).

[7] For background on Syria see Steven Heydemann, *Authoritarianism in Syria: Institutions and Social Conflict, 1946-1970* (Ithaca, NY: Cornell University Press, 1999); *Bassam Haddad, Business Networks in Syria: The Political Economy of Authoritarian Resilience* (Palo Alto, CA: Stanford University Press, 2012) and Fouad Ajami, *The Syrian Rebellion* (Stanford, CA: Hoover Institution Press, 2012).

[8] Mohammed Ayoob, "The New Cold War in the Middle East," *The National Interest*, January 16, 2013, http://nationalinterest.org/commentary/the-new-cold-war-the-middle-east-7974, and Fawaz Gerges, "Syrian hostilities bring Middle East catastrophe closer," CNN.com, May 6, 2013, http://edition.cnn.com/2013/05/06/opinion/opinion-gerges-syria

[9] This six-point plan outlines a set of guidelines and principles for a political transition in Syria. The full text is available at: http://

www.un.org/News/dh/infocus/Syria/FinalCommuniqueAction-GroupforSyria.pdf.

[10] Dmitri Trenin, "Syria: A Russian Perspective," *Sada*, June 28, 2012, http://carnegieendowment.org/2012/06/28/syria-russian-perspective/ccln.

[11] Aron Lund, *Syria's Salafi Insurgents: The Rise of the Syrian Islamic Front* (Stockholm: Swedish Institute for International Affairs, UI Occasional Paper no. 17, March 2013); Elizabeth O'Bagy, *Jihad in Syria* (Washington DC: Institute for the Study of War, Middle East Security Report 6, September 2012); Ben Hubbard, "Islamist Rebels Create Dilemma on Syria Policy," *New York Times*, April 27, 2013.

[12] See Michael Walzer, "The Argument about Humanitarian Intervention," *Dissent*, Winter 2002, pp. 29-37, among many articles and books.

[13] For a discussion of liberal internationalists who *opposed* the Iraq war, see Michael Bérubé, *The Left at War* (New York, NY: NYU Press, 2009), p. 146.

[14] Though many of the war's neocon proponents deployed humanitarian rhetoric, the 2003 invasion of Iraq was not a humanitarian intervention. Humanitarian interventions are limited to stopping mass atrocities in real time.

[15] Quoted in Mark Mazzetti, Eric Schmitt, and Erin Banco, "No Quick Impact in U.S. Arms Plan for Syria Rebels," *New York Times*, July 14, 2013, http://www.nytimes.com/2013/07/15/world/middleeast/no-quick-impact-in-us-arms-plan-for-syria-rebels.html.

[16] See Dexter Filkins, "The Thin Red Line: Inside the White House Debate over Syria," *The New Yorker*, May 13, 2013, 40-49.

[17] See, for example, Daniel Pipes, "Stay out of Syria: Intervention is a trap," *Washington Times*, August 20, 2012, www.washington-times.com/news/2012/aug/20/stay-out-of-syria; and Pipes, "The argument for Assad: If the Syrian regime falls now, worse rogues will win," *Washington Times*, April 11, 2013, www.washington-times.com/news/2013/apr/11/pipes-argument-assad

[18] For an example of the latter, see "Syria, intervention and the Arab revolution," an interview with Gilbert Achcar, author of *The People Want: A Radical Exploration of the Arab Uprising* (London: Saqi Books, 2013), at http://blip.tv/ecosocialism/syria-intervention-and-the-arab-revolution-6538205

Shadi Hamid

[19] Steven A. Cook, "It's Time to Think Seriously About Intervening in Syria," *The Atlantic*, January 17, 2012, www.theatlantic.com/international/archive/2012/01/its-time-to-think-seriously-about-intervening-in-syria/251468/

[20] Shadi Hamid, "Why We Have a Responsibility to Protect Syria," *The Atlantic*, January 26, 2012, www.theatlantic.com/international/archive/2012/01/why-we-have-a-responsibility-to-protect-syria/251908/

[21] Steven A. Cook, "Could a Syrian Intervention Work?" *The Atlantic*, March 2, 2012, www.theatlantic.com/international/archive/2012/03/could-a-syrian-intervention-work/253893/

[22] Shadi Hamid, "Lessons of the Libya Intervention," *The Atlantic*, August 22, 2011, www.theatlantic.com/international/archive/2011/08/lessons-of-the-libya-intervention/243922/

Michael Ignatieff

[23] On these themes, see Michael Ignatieff, *Blood and Belonging: Journeys into the New Nationalism* (New York: Penguin, 1993) and *The Warrior's Honor: Ethnic War and the Modern Conscience* (New York: Metropolitan, 1998).

[24] Richard Holbrooke, *To End A War* (New York: Random House, 1998)

[25] Stephen M. Walt, "The dearth of strategy on Syria," Foreign-Policy.com, March 21, 2013, http://walt.foreignpolicy.com/posts/2013/03/21/the_dearth_of_strategy_on_syria

[26] Leon Wieseltier, "Syria, Bosnia and the Old Mistakes," *The New Republic*, March 12, 2013, http://www.newrepublic.com/article/112605/syria-bosnia-and-old-mistakes. For the Obama interview, see Franklin Foer and Chris Hughes, "Barack Obama Is Not Pleased," *The New Republic*, January 27, 2013, http://www.newrepublic.com/article/112190/obama-interview-2013-sit-down-president.

[27] C. J. Chivers and Eric Schmitt, "Arms Airlift to Syria Rebels Expands, With Aid From C.I.A.," *New York Times,* March 24, 2013, http://www.nytimes.com/2013/03/25/world/middleeast/arms-airlift-to-syrian-rebels-expands-with-cia-aid.html.

Afra Jalabi

[28] I have changed the names of the activists inside Syria to protect their identities, but have not changed the names of the activists living outside Syria.

[29] The Day After project, an initiative of the United States Institute of Peace, is an international working group of Syrians representing a large spectrum of the country's opposition engaged in an independent transition planning process. See http://www. usip.org/the-day-after-project.

Anne-Marie Slaughter

[30] Anne-Marie Slaughter, "How to Halt the Butchery in Syria," *New York Times*, February 23, 2012, www.nytimes.com/2012/02/24/opinion/how-to-halt-the-butchery-in-syria.html

Tom Farer

[31] Howard LaFranchi, "Will Obama's new atrocities board lead to more Libya-style operations?" *Christian Science Monitor*, April 23, 2012, http://www.csmonitor.com/USA/Foreign-Policy/2012/0423/Will-Obama-s-new-atrocities-board-lead-to-more-Libya-style-operations

[32] Michel Seurat, *Syrie, l'Etat de barbarie* (Presses Universitaires de France, 2012).

[33] T.A. Frank, "Let Them Eat Kebabs: Why Asma Al Assad is the

perfect dictator's wife for the twenty-first century," *The New Republic*, April 25, 2013, www.newrepublic.com/article/112899/syrias-asma-al-assad-perfect-dicators-wife

Rafif Jouejati

[34] Shadi Hamid, "Why Is There a 'Red Line' on Chemical Weapons but Not on 70,000 Deaths?" *The Atlantic*, April 26, 2013, www.theatlantic.com/international/archive/2013/04/why-is-there-a-red-line-on-chemical-weapons-but-not-on-70-000-deaths/275328/

Marc Lynch

[35] Michael Doran, Salman Shaikh, "Arm the Syrian Rebels. Now." *Foreign Policy*, February 8, 2013, http://www.foreignpolicy.com/articles/2013/02/08/arm_the_syrian_rebels_now_assad_obama

[36] Kenneth M. Pollack, "How, When and Whether to End the War in Syria," *Washington Post*, August 10, 2012

[37] See Idean Salehyan, Kristian Skrede Gleditsch, and David E. Cunningham, "Explaining External Support for Insurgent Groups," *International Organization* Volume 65 Issue 04 October 2011, pp. 709-744.

[38] Steven Heydemann, "Managing militarization in Syria," ForeignPolicy.com, February 22, 2012, mideast.foreignpolicy.com/posts/2012/02/22/managing_militarization_in_syria; Salman Shaikh, "Losing Syria (And How to Avoid It)," Brookings Doha

Center Policy Briefing, October 18, 2012, www.brookings.edu/research/papers/2012/10/18-losing-syria-shaikh

[39] Marc Lynch, "The Syria debate, continued," ForegnPolicy.com, January 24, 2013, lynch.foreignpolicy.com/posts/2013/01/24/the_syria_debate_continued

[40] Robin Yassin-Kassab, "Fund Syria's Moderates," Foreign-Policy.com, January 23, 2013, www.foreignpolicy.com/articles/2013/01/23/fund_syria_s_moderates_rebels_civil_war

Nader Hashemi

[41] Stephen Zunes, "Syria: U.S. involvement could make things worse," *Santa Cruz Sentinel*, May 3, 2013, http://www.santa-cruzsentinel.com/opinion/ci_23169164/stephen-zunes-syria-u-s-involvement-could-make.

[42] See the contributions in this volume by Charles Glass, and Aslı Bâli and Aziz Rana. Also see Jonathan Steele, "Syria: How We Can End the Bloodshed," *The Guardian*, January 31, 2013, http://www.guardian.co.uk/commentisfree/2013/jan/31/syria-israel-attack-political-solution. For Noam Chomsky's views see Aida Edemariam, "Noam Chomsky: 'No individual changes anything alone'," *The Guardian*, March 22, 2013, http://www.guardian.co.uk/world/2013/mar/22/noam-chomsky-no-individual-changes-anything-alone.

[43] Human Rights Watch, *Syria's Tadmor Prison* (New York: Human Rights Watch, April 1, 1996). Available at: http://www.hrw.org/reports/1996/04/01/syrias-tadmor-prison.

[44] Human Rights Watch, *Torture Archipelago: Arbitrary Arrests, Torture and Enforced Disappearances in Syria's Underground Prisons Since March 2011* (New York: Human Rights Watch, July 3, 2012). Available at: http://www.hrw.org/news/2012/07/03/syria-torture-centers-revealed.

[45] According to figures provided by the Violations Documentation Center in Syria from March to August 2011. Available at: http://www.vdc-sy.info/index.php/en/.

[46] Amnesty International, *Crackdown in Syria: Terror in Kalakh* (London: Amnesty International, 2011), 19; Human Right Watch, *"We Live as in War": Crackdown on Protesters in Governorate of Homs* (New York: Human Rights Watch, 2011), 55-56; United National Human Rights Council, "Report of the independent international commission of inquiry on the Syrian Arab Republic," November 23, 2011, A/HRC/S-17/2/Add.1

[47] Nick Cumming-Bruce, "More Than 60,000 Have Died in Syrian Conflict, U.N. says," *New York Times*, January 2, 2013.

[48] See the dozens of reports by Amnesty International, Human Rights Watch and the UN Human Rights Council that chronicle the human rights catastrophe in Syria. On sexual violence see Lauren Wolfe, "Syria Has a Massive Rape Crisis," *The Atlantic*, April 3, 2013, http://www.theatlantic.com/international/archive/2013/04/syria-has-a-massive-rape-crisis/274583/.

[49] See Fergal Keane's interview with the boys from Deraa who launched the first protests. They explicitly reference the other Arab Spring revolts as a motivation. "Syria: The boys who

helped spark a revolution," BBC News, April 13, 2013, http://www.bbc.co.uk/news/world-middle-east-22140807.

[50] Rana Kabbani, "From the Turks to Assad: to us Syrians it is all brutal colonialism," *The Guardian*, March 29, 2011, http://www.guardian.co.uk/commentisfree/2011/mar/30/turks-assad-colonialism-family-mafia.

[51] Liam Stack, "In Sometimes Deadly Clashes, Defiant Syrians Protest," *New York Times*, April 17, 2011.

[52] Frank Barat, "Reframing the Israel-Palestine conflict," *New Internationalist*, April 1, 2011, http://newint.org/features/web-exclusive/2011/04/01/palestine-israel-interview-pappe/. Also see Rami Khouri, "The Long Revolt," *Wilson Quarterly* (Summer 2011), 43-46.

[53] Robert Fisk, "Truth and reconciliation?: It won't happen in Syria," *The Independent*, May 7, 2011.

[54] "'Friends of Syria' recognize opposition," *Al Jazeera* (English), December 12, 2012, http://www.aljazeera.com/news/middleeast/2012/12/201212124541767116.html.

[55] "The Position of NATO's Secretary General Regarding Intervention in Syria," Statement by the Syrian Coalition, April 24, 2013. http://www.etilaf.org/en/newsroom/press-release/item/433-the-position-of-nato%E2%80%99s-secretary-general-regarding-intervention-in-syria.html.

Thomas Pierret

[56] One of the best reports on these problems is Ghaith Abdul-Ahad, "How to Start a Battalion (in Five Easy Lessons)," *London Review of Books* 35, no. 4, 21 February 2013, 13-14, http://www.lrb.co.uk/v35/n04/ghaith-abdul-ahad/how-to-start-a-battalion-in-five-easy-lessons.

[57] On the role of private Salafi benefactors from Kuwait, see Elizabeth Dickinson, "Kuwait, 'the back office of logistical support' for Syria's rebels," *The National*, February 5, 2013, http://www.thenational.ae/news/world/middle-east/kuwait-the-back-office-of-logistical-support-for-syrias-rebels.

[58] C.J. Chivers and Eric Schmitt, "Saudis Step Up Help for Rebels in Syria With Croatian Arms," *New York Times*, February 25, 2013; Jonathan Dupree, "Syria Update: The Southern Battlefronts," *Institute for the Study of War*, April 5, 2013 (www.understandingwar.org/backgrounder/syria-update-southern-battlefronts).

[59] The Awakening Councils were militias that were recruited by the US and Iraqi governments among Sunni Arab tribes in order to fight al-Qaeda in the country. These tribesmen were often former allies of al-Qaeda and switched sides thanks to substantial financial incentives.

ACKNOWLEDGMENTS

A HUGE DEBT OF GRATITUDE IS OWED TO SEVERAL people who contributed in vital ways to this book's materialization.

Andrea Stanton, Assistant Professor of Religious Studies at the University of Denver and an affiliate faculty member of our Center for Middle East Studies (as well as the Newsletter Editor for the Syrian Studies Association), took part in several brainstorming/planning sessions for the conference on the Syrian crisis that we convened at the University of Denver in January 2013, out of which this book grew. She also chaired and served as a discussant for a particularly spirited session at the conference. Andrea's knowledge, contacts and suggestions have been invaluable to us. Douglas Garrison, the Research Assistant and Communications Director for our Center for Middle East Studies, has been instrumental at multiple stages. From his painstaking efforts organizing the conference to securing the rights to reprint several of the texts in this volume, from his diligent research on the crisis in Syria to skillfully editing the manuscript, Doug's fingerprints are all over this book.

Jeanne Mansfield, Assistant to the Editor of Boston Review, has adroitly managed the editorial production process. She has been enormously helpful and a pleasure to work with. We owe a special debt of gratitude to Deb Chasman and Joshua Cohen, *Boston Review*'s editors, for deciding to take this book on. We were keen on Boston Review Books being the publisher for this volume—with its commitment to thoughtful, critical debate about the essential questions of our time, we thought it a perfect fit. Deb was an ideal editorial interlocutor, providing well-judged suggestions that made the book stronger. It was a joy and also an honor to work with her on this book. Clay Morgan, Senior Acquisitions Editor at MIT Press, also provided helpful suggestions and nudged us in productive directions, for which we are grateful. Having this book published by MIT Press is nothing less than ideal.

CREDITS

"Syria Is Not Iraq" by Shadi Hamid first appeared online on *TheAtlantic*.com, February 4, 2013.

"Why There Is No Military Solution to the Syrian Conflict" by Aslı Bâli and Aziz Rana was written for this volume. It also appears (in slightly different form) on *Jadaliyya*.com, May 13, 2013.

"Bosnia and Syria: Intervention Then and Now" by Michael Ignatieff was written for this volume and appears here for the first time.

"What Should Be Done About the Syrian Tragedy?" by Richard Falk first appeared (in slightly different form) on his blog, *Citizen Pilgrimage*, as "On Syria: What to Do in 2013," January 19, 2013.

"Anxiously Anticipating a New Dawn: Voices of Syrian Activists" by Afra Jalabi was written for this volume and appears here for the first time.

"Syria Is Not a Problem from Hell—But If We Don't Act Quickly, It Will Be" by Anne-Marie Slaughter first appeared on *ForeignPolicy*.com, May 31, 2012.

"Supporting Unarmed Civil Insurrection in Syria" by Stephen Zunes first appeared, in longer form, on *ForeignPolicy*.com as "Supporting non-violence in Syria," December 20, 2012.

"A Syrian Case for Humanitarian Intervention" by Radwan Ziadeh was written for this volume and appears here for the first time.

"Syria: The Case for Staggered Decapitation" by Tom Farer was written for this volume and appears here for the first time.

"A Humanitarian Strategy Focused on Syrian Civilians" by Mary Kaldor was written for this volume. It also appears (in slightly different form) on *openDemocracy*.net as "Bordering on a New World War I," April 27, 2013.

"How to Ease Syrian Suffering" by Kenneth Roth first appeared in the *New York Times*, February 8, 2013.

"The Last Thing Syrians Need Is More Arms Going to Either Side" by Charles Glass first appeared in *The Guardian*, March 4, 2013.

"Syria Is Melting" by Rafif Jouejati was written for this volume and appears here for the first time.

"Shopping Option C for Syria" by Marc Lynch first appeared on *ForeignPolicy*.com, February 14, 2013.

"The Price of Inaction in Syria" by Christoph Reuter first appeared on *Spiegel Online International*, the English-language web edition of *Der Spiegel*, as "War without End: The Price of Inaction in Syria," April 4, 2013.

"With or Without Us: Why Syria's Future Is in Its Own Hands" by Fareed Zakaria first appeared in *TIME* as "With or Without Us," May 13, 2013.

"The Dangerous Price of Ignoring Syria" by Vali Nasr first appeared in the *New York Times* on April 15, 2013.

"Syria, Savagery and Self-Determination" by Nader Hashemi was written for this volume and appears here for the first time.

"From Dayton to Damascus" by Christopher R. Hill first appeared in the *New York Times* as "When to Talk to Monsters," May 15, 2013.

"Better Assad Than the Islamists?" by Thomas Pierret was written for this volume and appears here for the first time.

BOSTON REVIEW BOOKS

Boston Review Books is an imprint of *Boston Review*, a bimonthly magazine of ideas. The book series, like the magazine, covers a lot of ground. But a few premises tie it all together: that democracy depends on public discussion; that sometimes understanding means going deep; that vast inequalities are unjust; and that human imagination breaks free from neat political categories. Visit bostonreview.net for more information.